Melannie Svoboda, SND

everyday epiphanies

seeing the sacred in everything

TWENTY
THIRD *23rd*
PUBLICATIONS
www.23rdpublications.com

DEDICATION

To my brother John M. Svoboda:
he was an epiphany of God's faithful love.

Twenty-Third Publications
1 Montauk Avenue
Suite 200
New London, CT 06320
(860) 437-3012
(800) 321-0411
www.23rdpublications.com

ISBN: 978-1-58595-926-6
Library of Congress Catalog Card Number: 2013947410
Printed in the U.S.A.

Contents

Introduction

It happens every day.

You're brushing your teeth in the morning and the solution to a problem pops into your head. Or you're reading a familiar passage from Scripture and a certain word jumps out at you. Or you're sipping coffee with a friend and she says something that gives you a brand new way of looking at something.

Call these experiences what you will: moments of insight, inspiration, or grace. I call them mini-epiphanies. Strictly speaking, the word "epiphany" means an appearance or manifestation of God. In Scripture Moses experienced an epiphany when he encountered God in the burning bush and later when he met God amid thunder and lightning on Mt. Sinai. Our Christian feast of the Epiphany commemorates Christ's manifestation to the Magi as well as his manifestations at his baptism and the wedding feast of Cana. From the burning bush to the miracle at Cana—all are dramatic manifestations of God's presence in human lives.

Our mini-epiphanies, however, may not be that dramatic or earthshaking. They are more ordinary, more everyday. We experience these every time we delight in a simple pleasure, grow in understanding, learn a valuable lesson, or stand in awe before the unfathomable mystery of existence. Everyday epiphanies may seem insignificant, but, over time, they can produce vital changes in our awareness, attitude, and behavior.

This book is a collection of short reflections based on some of the everyday epiphanies in my own life. Although in one sense these are my epiphanies, I suspect that many of them will resonate with your own experience. After all, haven't we all watched children at play, enjoyed our friends, struggled with prayer, worried about someone we love? The reflections in this book focus on a wide range of topics such as love, beauty, family, nature, fear, pain, prayer. Many are directly rooted in Scripture. All conclude with a brief prayer.

Everyday Epiphanies is arranged in four parts: summer, fall, winter, spring. Seasonal reflections can be found under the respective season. Particular topics can be found in the index at the end of the book.

My hope in writing *Everyday Epiphanies* is simple: that we all might become more sensitive to the many subtle manifestations of God in our everyday lives—those instances when we suddenly feel we have brushed up against the Holy amid the ordinary events of daily life.

Summer

[1] **"Thy will be done"**

The paradigm of prayer is "Thy will be done." This is what Mary said at the Annunciation: "Let it be done unto me according to your word" (Lk 1:38). This is what Jesus prayed to Abba in the garden of Gethsemane: "Not my will but yours be done" (Lk 22:42). But it is good for us to remember that their prayer did not begin there.

Mary's prayer began in perplexity: "She was greatly troubled" (Lk 1:29). Then it moved into questioning: "How can this be?" (Lk 1:34). Only then did Mary pray "Thy will be done...." Similarly, Jesus began his prayer in Gethsemane by begging God "to remove this cup" (Lk 22:42). Only after that did he pray "Thy will be done."

Like the prayer of Mary and Jesus, our prayer may not always begin with "Thy will be done" either. It too may need to pass through other stages first. When struggles occur in our lives or something terrifying looms, we might have to sit in perplexity, ask God questions, and beg God to give us what we see as good. Only after doing that might we be able to say, "Thy will be done."

God, help me to be more accepting of whatever
form my prayer takes today.

⋯⋯⋯⋯⟨✷⟩⋯⋯⋯⋯

[2] **Little Hannah**

Little Hannah is four. Her brother Aaron, two. I notice Aaron's shoe is untied. "Come here, Aaron, and let me tie your shoe," I say. He comes, and I bend down and tie his shoe while Hannah watches closely. A few minutes later, Hannah comes to me with her pink sandal strap undone. "Do my shoe," she says, sticking her little foot out in front of me. I bend down and buckle it, smiling, for I know Hannah herself undid the strap so I would give her the same attention I had given her brother.

We are all little Hannahs. We all crave attention—from one another and (more importantly) from God. If only we would realize that, when it comes to getting God's attention, the attention is always there for the asking.

God, I place before you all that is "unbuckled" in my life.

---

[3] Making a personal investment in the game of life

To watch a baseball or football game without taking sides may be very relaxing, but it offers little excitement or fun.

The same is true for the more important contests in life—especially the primordial conflict between good and evil that is being played out before us right now on the fields of human history. I can ignore this conflict. I can just sit by and watch others struggling. Or I can take sides and become personally involved in that contest by making an investment in the outcome of that struggle—whether directly by my actions or indirectly by my counsel and prayers.

That's precisely what it means to be a Christian. It means being on the side of good. It means being on Jesus' team. It means making a personal investment with our lives toward the final outcome of human history.

Jesus, enable me to make a personal investment
on the side of the good today.

[4] **We know in wholes**

We know in wholes, but we realize in bits and pieces. We know, for example, that we are going to die. But we realize it only gradually. Perhaps we're in a near fatal accident. Or maybe we're suddenly faced with a serious illness. Or one day we bury a good friend our age. Only then do we realize in part what we already know in full: we are mortal. We are going to die.

Realization arrives late at life's party, only to discover that knowledge has been there the whole time.

God, help me to realize today what I already know.

---

[5] **Fringes will do**

During Mass today, I feel as if I'm standing on the outskirts or "fringes" of the congregation. I feel as if all the other people in the church are really present and fully attentive to what's going on at the altar, whereas I am only partly there, hovering at a distance. I don't like feeling this way. I want to feel completely at one with the sacred mystery. At dead center, so to speak.

My consolation every time this happens? The story of the woman with the hemorrhage (Lk 8:43–48). Her aim was simple enough: to touch but the tassels of Jesus' garment, the fringes. She told herself, "Touching them will be enough to heal me." So she did, and instantly, the woman was cured of her debilitating and embarrassing infirmity.

On days like today, this nameless woman reminds me of this great truth: when it comes to touching the holy—whether through liturgy or prayer or loving—fringes will do. For even the tassels of God's garment have the power to heal us of all our infirmities.

God, make me more aware of the ways today
I will touch your fringes.

---

[6] "Do you love me?"

"Do you love me?" This is the question Jesus asks Peter on the shore of the Sea of Galilee after Jesus' resurrection, and (more significantly) after Peter's betrayal (Jn 21:15). Jesus does not ask Peter:

"Do you know how to run a church?"
"Can you write a good encyclical?"
"How good are you at fundraising?"

No. Jesus asks, "Do you love me?" And if the disciple's answer to that question is "yes," then all the other things will fall into their proper place. If the answer is "no," however, the other things don't matter at all.

Jesus, may I always answer your question
"Do you love me?" with a resounding YES!

---

[7] Monosyllabic prayer

Sometimes our best prayer is monosyllabic: "God!" or "Help!" or "Why?" In the traditional English translation of the Our Father, there are only fifty-six words. And forty of them are monosyllabic: *our...be thy name...will be done on earth...give us this day...bread...lead us not.*

Maybe Jesus was trying to tell us something. When it comes to finding the right words in prayer, shorter is good, fewer is better. And don't all the great mystics of the church tell us this: the best prayer of all can be no words at all?

God, help me to pray with few and short words today —or maybe with no words at all.

---

[8] Things in heaven

A list of things we probably will not find in heaven: locks... clocks...handcuffs...scales...aspirin...erasers...parking meters... "for sale" signs...insurance policies...hearses... handkerchiefs...

God, give me a greater appreciation of heaven.

---

[9] Nicodemus

We are free to come to Jesus at any time: morning, noon, or night. But some of us, like Nicodemus, prefer to come at night (Jn 3:1–21). At night, when no one else can see us. At night, when everything is shrouded in darkness and we have lost our way. At night, when we can see nothing except the face of the Lord illumined by a tiny flicker of faith.

It would be bolder and certainly more dignified and self-satisfying to approach the Lord in broad daylight—in full view of others.

But Jesus overlooks our cowardice and sees only our coming.

Jesus, no matter what time of day it is in my life,
I want to say, "Lord, I'm coming!"

---

[10] **Frequently checking our email**

Being far away from home for any length of time can rattle
your self-confidence. You get this awful feeling that the farther
and longer you're away, the more the people back home aren't
missing you. And you fear they're realizing you aren't as important to them as they once thought you were. In fact, your family and friends are getting along quite well without you, thank
you, and the unique space you thought you occupied in their
lives is now being filled with other people and other interests.

You begin to think you mean nothing to them and you start
doubting your essential worth.

Little wonder you try to stay back this awful feeling of
insignificance by sending emails—a gesture to remind others of
your existence. Every email you send proclaims, "Look! It's me!
I'm still alive! And I'm remembering you! Are you remembering me?" And your frequent trips to your computer to check
your email are a source of embarrassment to yourself—one
more incontrovertible sign of your innate insecurity and your
desperate need to feel loved.

Your only consolation? You know a lot of other people frequently check their email too!

I need to feel remembered, God.

[11] **Emulating Emily**

Emily Dickinson was a gifted poet who generated hundreds
of poems, unique in form, profound in content. Her life is as
intriguing as her poetry. By age forty, Emily was a recluse.
Never married, though rumored to have been in love twice, she
seldom left her small house in Amherst.

Emily reminds us that we do not have to travel extensively
to grow in knowledge. We do not have to journey far to enjoy
rich experiences or gain wisdom. Knowledge sits in our own
backyard. Experience awaits us at our kitchen table. Wisdom is
as near as our fingertips.

Jesus, too, lived a life that some would call confined. The
Son of God was content to live his entire life within a relatively
small radius. Yet who would deny his expanse of knowledge,
his range of experience, his depth of wisdom?

If life denies us expansiveness, then let us opt for depth. For
every roadblock in one direction can be the impetus for growth
in another.

God, help me to find knowledge and wisdom
in my own backyard.

---

[12] **On loving hyenas**

I watched a National Geographic TV show on hyenas featuring
a scientist who has studied hyenas intensively for seven years.
The narrator said of this scientist, "He's probably the only
human being on earth who publicly admits, 'I love hyenas.'"

This scientist confirms two theories of mine: 1) If we study
anything long enough, we will eventually see goodness and

beauty—maybe where we previously thought none existed. 2) All loving begins with taking the time to know someone (or some thing!) better.

God, help me to take time today to know someone better.

---

[13] **What Jesus didn't say**

"What a bunch of mangy fishermen! No potential for leadership there, that's for sure!" (Mt 4:18–22).

"How many times must you forgive? Once seems more than enough to me" (Mt 18:22).

"A funeral? Back there in Nain? No, I didn't notice" (Lk 7:11–15).

"Me? Time for prayer? With all my responsibilities?" (Mk 1:35).

"Thanks, guys, for getting rid of those little brats. I don't have much use for kids" (Lk 18:15–17).

"Lady, take your alabaster jar and get out of here. You're embarrassing me! And put your veil back on your head, for heaven's sake!" (Mk 14:3–9).

"Take up your cushion and follow me" (Mt 16:24).

"Give to Caesar what belongs to Caesar—and that's just about everything!" (Mt 22:15–22)

"*Psst*, Judas! I'm sure we can cut a deal" (Jn 13:21–27).

Jesus, let me hear what you really said in the gospels—
and what you are really saying to me today.

[14] **Mrs. Siena**

St. Catherine of Siena did not get along with her mother, Lapa. As one biographer put it, "Lapa loved Catherine dearly but understood her not at all."

Lapa was, by any standards, an extraordinary woman. She gave birth to twenty-five children (yes, twenty-five!), of which Catherine was the twenty-fourth. The teen years were especially strained for both mother and daughter. Lapa was always nagging Catherine to pay more attention to her appearance so she might snare a well-to-do husband. But Catherine had other ambitions, namely, to be a nun.

One day, when the fifteen-year-old Catherine was feeling particularly ascetical, she chopped off most of her beautiful golden-brown hair. To conceal the deed from her mother, she donned a small white cap. Suspicious, Lapa snatched off the cap and shrieked in horror, "What have you done?! How could you do this to me?!"

Lapa and Catherine. Their story is consoling for any of us who find ourselves at odds with those we love. Relationships can be stressful—even for saints!

God, help me to be more patient today with those I love.

---

[15] **Faith and fun**

Sometimes we Christians are too grim. We measure our faith by our ability to suffer and do penance. But our ability to endure is only half the measure of our faith. The other half is our ability to enjoy. After all, don't all the Beatitudes begin with the word "happy"?

Similarly, the Talmud says that a person will be called to account on judgment day for every permissible thing he or she might have enjoyed, but did not. Interesting concept: God actually wants us to enjoy things! God wants us to have fun!

At the end of each day, maybe we should ask ourselves, "What did I enjoy today? How much fun did I have?"

God, increase my ability to enjoy and my capacity to have fun.

---

[16] Writing is a lot like praying

Writing is a lot like praying. I write because I feel I have to, I want to. I pray for the same reasons: I have to, I want to. But this doesn't mean I feel like writing (or praying) every day. Some days I do. (Praise God!) But some days I don't.

Some days I have to make myself write. This means I almost have to force myself to sit at my computer and write. It's the same with my prayer. Some days I have to force myself to pray.

Why bother? Why bother to write or pray on days I don't feel like doing either?

I bother because I've learned this: incredible things can happen precisely on those days I don't feel like writing or praying. I've learned that wonderful things can occur when I push myself beyond my immediate inclination. When I make myself write, who knows? A poem or paragraph may come gushing out, one I never knew was inside me. And when I push myself to pray, who knows? I may just run smack into the living, breathing, charming, challenging, loving God!

God, for all those times I feel like praying, I say,

"Thank you." And for all those times I don't feel like praying, I say, "Please help me to push myself beyond my immediate inclination and risk meeting you."

---

[17] **A sense of humor**

Of all the gifts we could have, the most valuable might be a sense of humor. In fact, given the option, most of us would probably choose a sense of humor over other gifts such as superior intelligence, good looks, athletic prowess, or even good health.

Why? Because without a sense of humor, we might be tempted to take ourselves and those other gifts too seriously. And with a sense of humor, we can get along fairly well without those other gifts. So we're no Einstein; at least we can laugh at our mistakes. So we're no beauty; we can chuckle at our imperfect body. So we're not in perfect health; we can still smile.

I wonder: can we have genuine faith without also having a sense of humor? Don't the two go hand in hand? Faith gives us a broader vision of life. So does a sense of humor. Faith enables us to trust in the essential goodness of life. So does humor. Faith helps us to keep things in perspective. So does humor.

In fact, one measure of the wholeness of our faith may be the healthiness of our sense of humor.

God, nourish my sense of humor today.

[18] **The Bible is not escapist literature**

The Bible is not escapist literature. It does not avoid evil. In fact, it has a heck of a lot of sin in it. Why? Because the world has a heck of a lot of sin in it! And if the Bible teaches us anything, it is this: how to live a good life in the real world, a world filled with a lot of goodness, yes, but a world also choking in sin.

We read the Bible, therefore, not solely to be consoled: "I'm okay, you're okay. Aren't we wonderful?" We read the Bible also to be challenged: "I'm not okay. You're not okay. What are we doing about that?"

God, help me to be open to both the
consolations and challenges of the Bible.

[19] **Honesty and caring**

Sometimes we confuse honesty with caring. "I'm just being honest with you," we say after lambasting someone. Or, "It's the truth," we say to justify our insensitive remarks.

Honesty and caring are not the same. You can have honesty without caring, but you can't have caring without honesty. Why is this so? Because caring is honesty plus, and the plus is always this: "I love you." Honesty without the reassurance of this love is not caring at all, and it can do more harm than good. In fact, honesty without love can be a form of violence.

God, help me to be loving in my honesty today.

[20] **Learning obedience through beauty**

Anne Morrow Lindbergh wrote that she used to think we came to true knowledge through suffering. But later she believed that we learn "through suffering and beauty. One alone won't do it."

In the letter to the Hebrews we find these words: "(Jesus) learned obedience through what he suffered" (Heb 5:8). But if what Lindbergh says is true, did Jesus also learn obedience through beauty?

I think so. The gospels tell us that Jesus was sensitive to beauty, all kinds of beauty. Like many of us, he appreciated the beauty in nature. Jesus sometimes stood and gazed off into the distance, sensing intuitively a vista's power to calm or inspire, whether the vista included bobbing lilies, golden wheat fields, a bustling city, or a glistening sea. From his words, we know Jesus was attuned to the beauty of changing weather and seasons, both subtle and dramatic. As a carpenter, he appreciated beautiful wood. As a human being, he delighted in a good meal. After all, he was labeled a glutton!

Jesus appreciated the beauty of animals, too, and incorporated many of them into his teachings: sheep, goats, cattle, camels, wolves, swine, snakes, doves, fish, chickens, and even dogs.

But it was primarily in his dealings with people that Jesus came to know and appreciate beauty: the beauty of parents' devotion to their children, a Roman centurion's concern for his slave, a cured leper's gratitude, a poor widow's generosity, a friend's loyalty.

Yes, Jesus learned obedience through suffering; but he also came to know and embrace God's will through beauty.

Jesus, help me to learn obedience through
both suffering and beauty.

[21] Hobo signs

Years ago, hobos had the custom of leaving messages for one another along the road. Devising their own system of symbols, they scrawled these messages with chalk on fenceposts, barns, train stations, and other places. A simple cross, for example, meant "angel food" and indicated a place that offered temporary shelter and a free meal—provided you sat through a sermon first. A triangle with upraised arms marked a home where the owner had a gun. A sketch that resembled a comb warned of a mean dog with sharp teeth.

We Christians are something like those hobos, for we, too, are on a journey far from home. Wending our way on earth, we know that both dangers and opportunities lie around us. But we need help to discern which is which. We need signs to steer us clear of mean dogs and to direct us to temporary housing and free meals. Fortunately, other "hobos" have gone before us and helped mark the way, most notably the saints. Their lives as well as their writings are like messages scrawled in chalk helping to guide us to our eternal home.

God, make me more attentive to the messages
your saints have scrawled for me.

---

[22] Two kids on a slide

I glanced out my window yesterday afternoon and saw two small children on the playground below. The little girl was about eight; the boy (her little brother, I concluded) was about three. The girl had just finished going down the slide. Having watched her, the little boy began to climb the steps, while his sister stood at the end of the slide waiting.

The higher the boy climbed, the slower he went, obviously afraid. Yet, with his sister yelling words of encouragement, the boy continued to climb. Arriving at the top, he sat down gingerly. His sister, holding wide her arms to receive him, encouraged him to slide down. For a few seconds, the boy sat poised there. Then suddenly he gave himself a big push. In a flash he was down the slide and crashing into his sister below. The impact almost knocked her over, but somehow she managed to keep herself—and her little brother—from falling over.

How much we rely on the encouragement of others to do the hard things in life. If it hadn't been for his sister, that little boy probably would never have gone down that slide. He needed his sister's example and her encouragement. He also needed her presence at the end of the slide, waiting with open arms to catch him.

Jesus goes before us. And he waits for us—with open arms—at the end of our slide.

Jesus, you encourage me to do the hard things in life by waiting for me with open arms.

[23] **Mary's prayer at Cana**

Mary's request at the wedding feast of Cana reminds us that we do not have to resort to explanations when we ask God for things. We need not go into detail. Sometimes a simple statement of fact will do.

"They have no wine," Mary says (Jn 2:3). Having stated that, she leaves everything else in Jesus' hands.

Sometimes our prayer can be like that: "So-and-so is ill…People are hurting…I'm really worried about X…I'm lonely…."

Just state the fact and let Jesus act.

Of course, we must be willing to accept the action Jesus takes, even when he appears to take no action at all, or (just as difficult) when he appears to be asking *us* to take an action we're reluctant to take.

Jesus, let my prayer be simple statements of fact today, and help me to accept whatever action you decide to take.

---

[24] Midsummer's Day dialogues

June 22 is the time of the summer solstice in the northern hemisphere. It is also known as "Midsummer's Day." According to legend, this is the time of year when the veil that separates the various life forms on earth is the thinnest, making communication between them the easiest.

This is the day when Ms. Dandelion can dialogue with Mr. Worm, when Herr Goose can chat with Old Man Willow, and when human beings can converse effortlessly with the stars. Believing this to be true, I go outside this afternoon to dialogue with other life forms—and the so-called "inanimate" forms as well—asking them to share their wisdom with me.

I come to a herd of cows standing under some trees at the edge of the pasture. "Good afternoon, Lady Cows," I say. "Would you mind sharing some of your wisdom with me?"

"Keep your fanny to the wind," says the first cow.

"Never wander too far from the herd," says the second.

"If it's hot—like today—seek shade," says a third.

"The flies are terrible," says another as she swishes her tail back and forth and all around. "But tails and ears do help. And don't think it's beneath your dignity to rub up against Brother

Tree at times or to lumber into Sister Creek. And, over the years, we cows have learned this little trick to get relief from the flies: we stand head to tail with our fellow cows. When we do this, we can take advantage of our sisters' swatting tails to get rid of those pesky flies that neither our own ears nor our own tail can reach."

"Ruminate, ruminate, ruminate," says another cow as she chews her cud contentedly.

"Thank you for your wisdom, Lady Cows," I say as I start to walk away. "I'll ruminate, ruminate, ruminate on everything you've said to me." And I do.

God, lead me to ruminate on nature's wisdom today.

---

[25] Dialogue with Grandpa Willow Tree

I seek out Grandpa Willow standing near the edge of Sister Creek. With his massive trunk and gnarled branches, he is more stump now than towering tree. Yet dozens of lush green branches sprout from his broken limbs and torso.

"Greetings, Grandpa Willow," I say. "Would you please share your wisdom with me today?"

Effortlessly Grandpa Willow begins to share his wisdom with me. He speaks slowly, in short, declarative sentences, the language of the truly wise.

"Every knot's a story," he says. "Every gnarl's a blessing. One day at a time. Perseverance comes mostly from within. Stay close to your water supply. Be generous with your branches and your shade. Bend, bend, bend. Broken branches are a matter of course: don't fret their loss. New ones are sure to sprout in their place. Look at all of mine!" and he shakes his new growth in the breeze.

I thank Grandpa Willow for his bountiful wisdom and, reluctantly, I take my leave.

God, help me to absorb some of Grandpa Willow's wisdom.

---

[26] A Hasidic story

A father complained to the baalshem that his son had forgotten God. "What, Rabbi, should I do?" he asked. The baalshem answered, "Love him more than ever."

It was columnist Erma Bombeck who wrote something similar: it is when our children deserve our love the least that they need it the most.

God, help me to see who needs my love the most today.

---

[27] Only God?

At the end of the book of Micah we find this beautiful prayer:
Shepherd your people with your staff, the flock that belongs to you....Who is a God like you, pardoning iniquity and passing over the transgression of the remnant of your possession?...(You) delight in showing clemency. (You) will again have compassion upon us....You will cast all our sins into the depths of the sea. (MI 7:14, 18–19)
What makes this prayer so noteworthy are the circumstanc-

es under which it was composed. It was written right after the chosen people returned from their exile in Babylon, one of the lowest points in their history. They had been totally humiliated by their enemy, their numbers had been decimated, and their land was taken away. In short, they were a people without hope and without a future. Yet they could pray a prayer filled with total trust in God's goodness and mercy.

In one way, this is remarkable. But in another way, it is not. For, at this low point in their history, the people had nothing left to trust in. Their numbers, land, power, and potential had all been taken away. They had only God.

Only God? Sometimes our prayer is at its best when our lives are at their worst.

God, I will trust you today—only you.

---

[28] **Jesus did not carry a pocket calendar**

Jesus did not carry a pocket calendar. He did not wear a watch. He didn't say, "Sorry, Lazarus. I can't make it Friday evening. Board meeting." Or, "Sorry, Martha, Mary. Saturday's out. I have to write those Beatitudes, you know."

When the women brought their children to Jesus for a blessing, he didn't look at his watch and say, "Well, okay, let the little children come to me, but only for five minutes." And when Nicodemus came to him at night, Jesus didn't say, "Look, Nick, it's after ten. Can't you come during regular office hours?"

How free are *we* in relating to others? Do we put too much stock in efficiency? Do we run our families, personal relationships, and parishes like corporate businesses?

Dates are important. Appointments are necessary. Order has its place. But do we allow them to rule our relationships?

Jesus, help me to be freer in relating to others today.

------------------ ❖ ------------------

[29] Accepting both talents and limitations

We must learn to accept both our talents and our limitations. Ironically, it is sometimes easier for us to accept the latter than the former. Why? In accepting our limitations we are left off the hook, so to speak. Saying "I can't draw a straight line with a ruler" releases us from any obligation to draw. The statement "I can't dance" allows us to sit complacently beside the dance floor.

Talents, on the other hand, call us to action, to service. You can write, cook, or sing? Then shouldn't you be using these gifts in the service of others?

Talents are not the opposite of limitations. Most so-called talented individuals work very hard at what they do. Professional ice skaters, for example, take to the ice every day, show or no show. Professional athletes spend many hours off the field in the weight room. Writers devote hours to research and rewriting. In other words, so-called talented people are always pushing themselves beyond the limitations of time, energy, and innate skill.

A good question to ask ourselves is this: are we too quick to accept as a limitation what may be the outer edge of a latent talent?

God, help me to use one of my talents today
in the service of others.

[30] **Sensitivity: the art of the small**

Sometimes sensitivity seems more cross than gift. "If I weren't so sensitive," we reason, "I wouldn't feel this pain." Even though sensitivity can cause pain, it is a gift that is absolutely essential for Christian living. After all, most of the good that is done in the world is the direct result of somebody's sensitivity.

Carlos Valles, SJ, calls sensitivity "the art of the small." He maintains that, ordinarily, sensitivity is not expressed in sweeping movements, but in little gestures: the attentive look, the kind interpretation, the simple word, the small token, and the gentle touch.

Jesus was sensitive. He worked his first miracle at a wedding reception to save a young couple from embarrassment (Jn 2:1–11). While being mobbed by a crowd, Jesus was sensitive to the tassel-touching of the woman with the hemorrhage (Lk 8:43–48). And standing outside the temple treasury that one day, Jesus seemed to be the only one to notice the poor widow toss in her two small coins—and he instantly assessed their real worth (Mk 12:41–44).

We need never apologize or feel bad for being sensitive. Jesus himself was master of this art of the small.

Jesus, help me to be sensitive today,
to master this art of the small, like you.

---

[31] **The ministry of conversation**

The gospels frequently show Jesus conversing with people. When the two disciples of John the Baptist meet Jesus for the first time, they ask him, "Rabbi, where are you staying?" Jesus replies, "Come and you will see" (Jn 1:38–39). The two men go with Jesus and spend the entire day with him. What did the three men do together that day if not engage in conversation?

Something similar happens to the man in the land of the Gerasenes who was possessed by demons. After he was cured by Jesus, the man sits down and converses with Jesus (Lk 8:35). Other individuals in the gospels were also changed for the better simply by having a good conversation with Jesus: Nicodemus, Zacchaeus, the woman at the well, Mary and Martha, the disciples on the road to Emmaus, to name a few.

Today we tend to think of evangelization in terms of teaching and preaching, that is, in terms of talking to people or, worse yet, talking *at* people. But Jesus shows us another way: the art of conversation. Jesus did teach and preach, of course, but he also spent considerable time simply talking with people—asking them questions, listening to their stories, and sharing his own thoughts and feelings with them.

If we wish to become more effective evangelizers, then maybe we have to reclaim the art of conversation.

Jesus, teach me the ministry of conversation.

---

[32] The chaplain at the children's hospital

Sister Rose is a chaplain at a children's hospital. Every day she ministers to sick and dying children and their families. In the morning she holds the hand of Troy, a four-year-old swathed in bandages in the burn unit. As she leaves the unit, a nurse whispers to her, "He's not going to make it."

At noon she cradles a sobbing mother, Carmelita, whose ten-year-old daughter has just been diagnosed with leukemia.

And right before leaving, she helps two stunned parents with the funeral arrangements for their daughter, age five, who ran out in front of a car.

And when Sister Rose comes home tonight, one of us greets her with "You're late." Another one complains, "The coffee maker's not working again." And the third one asks, "Isn't this rain depressing?"

God, help me to keep things in perspective today.

---

[33] The roar of the ordinary

One of the greatest gifts God has given me is my love for the ordinary. Vanilla ice cream, daisies, and even a glass of water often bring me just as much joy and pleasure as baked Alaska, long-stemmed red roses, and fine French wine.

I feel sorry for people who overlook the ordinary, who don't appreciate the everyday, who need the exotic to experience pleasure. In her novel *Middlemarch*, George Eliot writes, "If we had a keen vision and a feeling of all ordinary human life, it would be like hearing the grass grow and the squirrel's heart beat, and we should die of that roar which lies on the other side of silence."

Happy are they who have a keen feel for everyday human life, whose ears are attuned to the roar of the ordinary. Happy are they who get a kick out of the commonplace, for they shall encounter joy and pleasure wherever they go!

God, increase in me a love for the ordinary.

[34] **Jesus saves**

One of the first controversies in the early church is recorded in Acts. It seems that certain individuals were teaching, "Unless you are circumcised according to the custom of Moses, you cannot be saved" (Acts 15:1). The apostles and elders finally had to meet in Jerusalem t settle the matter.

Peter and others strongly opposed the view that converts to Christianity had to submit to circumcision. "We believe that we will be saved through the grace of the Lord Jesus," Peter said emphatically. In other words, Jesus saves—and not a specific law or ritual. In the end, Peter's thinking prevailed.

At first glance this ancient controversy may seem pretty tame to us and a far cry from the controversies in the current church. But is it really? Don't we continue to struggle with the same underlying question: who (or what) saves us? Aren't we still tempted to substitute other things for Jesus?

What things? Here are a few: Virtue saves. Education saves. Obedience saves. A certain method of prayer saves. A specific way of celebrating liturgy saves. This theologian saves. Gender saves. Liberalism saves. Conservatism saves. Or even: I save myself!

Maybe we need to hear Peter's words again today: "We will be saved through the grace of the Lord Jesus."

Jesus, strengthen my conviction that you alone are my savior.

---

[35] **Geese are not dumb**

A man was outside in his yard raking leaves with his little boy. Suddenly a flock of wild geese flew overhead, on their way south for the winter. "Look at the geese!" the man called to his son. "See how they're flying in a vee?"

The boy stared up in amazement. "Wow!" he exclaimed. Then he asked his father, "Do they know any other letters?"

We smile at the little boy's remark. Of course geese don't know any other letters. When it comes to knowing the alphabet, geese are dumb! But when it comes to other things, geese are very smart. After all, most of them know how to migrate thousands of miles each year. And they make the trek without map, compass, or suitcase and without benefit of restaurants and motels along the way. And somewhere in their past, geese figured out the laws of physics—at least enough to know how to conserve energy by flying in a V-formation.

St. Francis of Assisi, believing all creation was holy, even called animals his brothers and sisters. Animals have much to teach us if we let them.

God, help me to know my animal brothers and sisters better so that I may learn from them.

---

[36] Wait and see

Someone has said that when it comes to deciding whether or not to do something, we have three choices: 1) Do it. 2) Delegate it. 3) Ditch it. But isn't there a fourth? Delay it. In other words, do nothing and wait and see. Some might say that doing nothing or waiting around is procrastination, and procrastination is unhealthy.

But not all delaying is procrastination. Not all waiting is unhealthy. Jesus himself encouraged waiting. In his parable of the wheat and the weeds, for example, he cautions against rushing madly into a field of wheat to yank out all the weeds (Mt 13:24–30). "Wait until the harvest," he urges. "Lest you pull up the precious wheat with the weeds."

As Christians, there are times we will be called to act—that is, to do it, delegate it, or ditch it. But such actions must always be balanced with our willingness to wait and see.

God, teach me to wait and see.

---

[37] George Dawson, ninety-eight

George Dawson of Dallas, the grandson of a slave, attended school for the first time at age ninety-eight. What prompted him to start school so late in life? "I was lost in a sea of words," he explained. "And I wanted to read my Bible."

George Dawson reminds us that we are never too old to learn something new. A nun friend of mine learned to swim at age seventy. Another friend started her writing career at age seventy-six. And Grandma Moses was almost eighty when she started to paint. Even in the Bible we have the example of Abraham who, at seventy, was called by God to start a whole new life in a brand new land.

The philosopher Martin Buber said it well: "To be old is a glorious thing when one has not unlearned what it means 'to begin.'"

God, help me to begin something new today.

[38] God's good company
Why do we pray?

For many reasons, I'm sure. But the basic reason, I think, is this: we pray to put ourselves in the presence of Someone who is absolutely favorably disposed toward us. Quite simply, we pray in order to be with Someone who loves us, delights in us, and thinks the world of us. Namely, God.

Think of it in human terms. We go to a big party and step into a room filled with people. To whom do we gravitate? To Joe Blow over there, who doesn't like us? To Hector What's-his-name over there, who barely knows us? Or to Sally Clapsaddle over there, who's known us for years and really, really likes us? The answer is obvious: we head for Sally.

When we go to prayer, we are seeking out Someone who has known us forever and likes us more than any other person does or could. Why would we not eagerly seek out such good company? Why do we not run to prayer?

God, thank you for your good company!

---

[39] Solving problems with a harp
One of my favorite lines in the psalms is this: "I will solve my riddle to the music of the harp" (Ps 49:4). Another translation says, "I will solve my problem with the music of a harp."

That verse from the psalm is a good one to call to mind whenever we are beset with riddles or problems in life. Do we ever let music help us to work through our difficulties?

Most of us instinctively reach for reason to solve our problems. We think, we examine, we analyze. In addition, we often seek the advice of others, going from person to person to try to find someone who will solve our problem for us. Or we may seek solutions on the Internet or in a book. Though these ways may be helpful, we might want to imitate the psalmist and try music.

Listening to music can ease our minds and soothe our hearts—which just might help us to solve our problems more easily, or at least to face them with greater patience and trust. Listening to or singing religious songs might be particularly helpful in directing us to some action or in simply reminding us of God's everlasting love.

"I will solve my problem with a harp"—or piano, or guitar, or flute, or saxophone, or complete orchestra, or even by singing slowly and softly, "Amazing grace, how sweet the sound...."

God, help me to make time for music today.

---

[40] **Writing a book**

Writing a book is a lot like having a baby. (Being a nun, I've never had a baby, but I have "had" several books.) First, there's that moment of conception. Conception can happen at any time—even when you don't expect. I conceived the idea for one of my books while blow-drying my hair in the bathroom!

Next comes the pregnancy. Working on a book has its own version of morning sickness: words won't come, ideas dry up, you get discouraged and depressed, and all the while you realize that a new and independent life is growing inside of you, growing because of you and, simultaneously, growing despite you. Then there's all the care you take to foster this new life—the people you seek out for encouragement and advice, the research you do. Other individuals are also involved in the development of your unborn child. Friends, editors, and proof-readers act as doctors and midwives. Seeing the proofs of your book is a lot like viewing a sonogram, for that's when you first catch a glimpse of your baby's shape and form.

There are labor pains throughout the writing process: the endless rewriting, the tedious proofreading, the meticulous attention to detail. Finally, the moment of birth arrives. I treasure that moment when the small box arrives from my publisher containing several advance copies of my book. I ritualize the opening of the box with prayer, thanking God for everyone who helped me to bring forth this child, and asking God to bless everyone who will eventually read this book. Finally, I open the box, pick up a copy of my book, examine it lovingly, and press it to my heart with gratitude and joy.

Writing a book is like giving birth. So are a lot of other worthwhile things.

*God, make me more attentive to whatever
I am giving birth to in my life.*

---

[41] Jesus never said, "I told you so!"

...and it's not because he didn't have ample opportunity, either. When he arrives at the home of Jairus, for example, he is told that Jairus' daughter is already dead. Jesus says to the mourners gathered there, "The child is not dead but sleeping" (Mk 5:39). Hearing this, the crowd laughs at Jesus. We all know what happens next. Jesus raises the little girl from the dead and, instead of saying to the crowd, "See, I told you so!" he says to her parents, "Give her something to eat."

Another time Jesus could have said "I told you so!" was after the resurrection when the apostles were cowering in the upper room. Jesus suddenly appears in their midst and says to them, "Peace be with you." Then he commissions them: "As the Father has sent me, so I send you" (Jn 20:19–21). Later, on the shore of the Sea of Galilee, Jesus singles out Peter, the one person to whom he had every right to say, "See? I told you you would betray me! I told you I would rise!" But instead, Jesus asks, "Simon, son of John, do you love me?" And when Peter humbly professes his love, Jesus says, "Feed my sheep" (Jn 21:16–17).

The lesson is clear. Instead of saying "I told you so" to individuals who were proven wrong, Jesus gave them a second chance. By entrusting them with a new responsibility, he offered them the opportunity to reclaim their self-esteem and to prove anew their love.

God, help me to give someone a second chance today.

---

[42] **We know who holds the future**

There is probably nothing we humans fear more than the future. Just look at how many office buildings in this country belong to insurance companies. The viability of so many companies is directly attributable to our basic fear of tomorrow, a fear that causes us to spend billions of dollars each year trying to insure ourselves against minor setbacks or major catastrophes.

This fear of the future also explains our fascination with those individuals who claim to be able to predict the future. If anyone really could predict the future with any degree of accuracy, he or she would be worshiped as a god.

How do we face this unknown and often foreboding future with any degree of equilibrium? By trusting in God. For God is not only the God of the past and the present; God is also the God of the future. The old maxim says it well: "We don't know what the future holds, but we know who holds the future." Or another one: "Don't be afraid of tomorrow. God is already there."

God, may I entrust all my fears of the future to you,
the One who holds the future.

---

[43] Quotes on friendship

One does not make friends. One recognizes them.
❁ GARTH HENRICHS

If you want an accounting of your worth, count your friends.
❁ MERRY BROWNE

No matter what accomplishments you achieve,
someone helps you. ❁ ALTHEA GIBSON

True happiness consists not in the multitude of friends,
but in their worth and choice. ❁ BEN JONSON

A true friend never gets in your way unless you
happen to be going down. ❁ ARNOLD GLASOW

Thank you, God, for my friends.
Help me to reach out to one of them today.

[44] **Heaven is coming home**

On my way home from the meeting, I decide to stop in to see Mom and Dad. It's a cold, dark November evening. Suppertime. As I pull into the driveway, I see lights on in the kitchen. Through the window I spot Dad in his red plaid flannel shirt, sitting at the table with his newspaper. Mom, aproned, is standing by the stove stirring something—homemade leek soup, perhaps. Dad, catching sight of me through the window, smiles and stands up stiffly and slightly stooped. As I step up onto the back porch, Dad opens the door wide and announces cheerfully, "Well, look who's here!" And I step into the warmth of that kitchen and into the warmth of their embraces.

That's what it's going to be like when I die and enter heaven. It will be like stepping out of the cold and darkness, into the warmth and brightness of a homey kitchen, with Mom and Dad there waiting for me. And they will both smile when they see me and open wide their arms. And Dad will announce cheerfully, "Well, look who's here!"

God, may I keep before myself a clear,
strong image of entering heaven.

---

[45] **What's wrong with God**

Sometimes I say to God: "You know what's wrong with you?"

And God asks, "What?"

And I begin to enumerate. "You love too indiscriminately. You trust people way too much. You're far too forgiving. And you're entirely too patient!"

Having said that, I invite God to tell me what's wrong with

me. But all I hear God say is, "You know, Honey, I really get a kick out of you!"

Which only proves my point.

God, thank you for loving me so much.

---

[46] The popular cow

A certain farmer had a cow that was very much loved by his family and neighbors. He also had a pig that wasn't as popular. One day the pig said to the cow, "How come everybody likes you so much? People say you're generous because you give milk, butter, and cream every day. Heck! I give more than that. I give bacon and ham. And you can even pickle my feet! Yet, I'm not as popular as you are. Why?"

Said the cow, "Maybe it's because I give while I'm still alive."

What we give after we're dead means little. What really counts is what we give of ourselves, how much we love, while we're still alive.

God, help me to give of myself to others today
—while I'm still alive.

---

[47] The promise of ultimate victory

Jesus promises us ultimate victory—the victory of life over death, good over evil, joy over sorrow. Victory, ultimate victory. But what exactly is meant by ultimate victory? It means final victory, conclusive victory, in-the-end victory. Victory not necessarily today or even tomorrow. But eventually. And finally.

Belief in the promise of ultimate victory should affect the way we live our lives in the present. An analogy might be helpful. Let's say we play on a football team. Our team, 2–8, is playing a crucial game against a formidable opponent, 10–0. Let's say that before the game our team learns—with absolute certainty—that we are going to win this game. For sure! No doubt about it!

How would such knowledge affect our playing? Some might say it would make us lethargic. "If we know we're going to win, why put forth any effort?" Possibly. But not probably. I think such knowledge would fire us up. It would increase our courage and self-confidence, thus enabling us to play better than ever perhaps.

But let's say, at the end of the first quarter we're down 14–0. Would we be discouraged? Not really. Knowledge of the final victory would help to keep us in the game. In fact, if at half time we were down 31–0, we might find ourselves saying things like this: "Down by 31—yet we're going to win? Incredible! I can't wait to play the second half to see how we pull this one out!" Or, "Down by 31! We've gotta get some incredible breaks to turn this one around. Lady Luck's gotta start smiling on us! After all, we can't do it ourselves. We're not that good. We've shown that!"

And that's exactly true. In order to win we would need some breaks. Perhaps the opposing quarterback dislocates his shoulder and has to leave the game. Maybe their defense, overly confident because of their 31-point lead, starts to get sloppy and begins to make all kinds of fundamental mistakes. And maybe our kicker is aided by a favorable wind, the football takes a few crazy bounces in our favor, and our quarterback throws a successful Hail Mary pass in the end zone. Whatever, we play the game with energy and enthusiasm, using the limited skills we have, relying on other forces to help us, confident in the knowledge of ultimate victory, and what happens? We finally do win the game—in overtime—34–31. Ultimate victory!

In the game of life, Jesus promises us ultimate victory: life over death, goodness over evil, joy over sorrow. Maybe at this moment we don't feel close to victory. In fact, maybe we're down by 14 or even 31. But our belief in Jesus' promise keeps us in the game—to the end. We play with courage and enthusiasm, using what limited skills we have, and trusting not in our own power, but in the power of Jesus who assures us that ultimate victory will be ours!

Jesus, strengthen my belief in your promise of ultimate victory, and may that belief affect the way I live this day.

---

[48] Temporary friendships

There's something in us that wants friendships to last forever. And miraculously, some do. Some friendships manage to weather the floods and droughts of everyday living, to negotiate the unexpected turns and hairpin curves of two separate lives—and last a lifetime. For these, we thank God.

But what about those other friendships that last for only a time? Those that gradually fade away or abruptly and painfully end? Can we thank God for these, too?

I think we can. For even temporary friendships bequeath to us memories and gifts that cannot be taken away even once the friendship has ended. Furthermore, just because a friendship ends doesn't mean it wasn't a blessing—at least for a certain period of our lives. Some friendships end because the two friends grow apart. These endings, as painful as they may be, call us to respect both ourselves and the other person, for we know we cannot continue in a relationship that does violence to either party. Some broken relationships tell us that the best thing we can say to some individuals is "goodbye." When we do this, we're acknowledging humbly that our friendship is not meant for everyone.

The poet John Donne wrote, "No (one) is an island," but Anne Morrow Lindbergh disagreed when she wrote, "We are all islands in a common sea." Temporary friendships underscore the great truth of our basic "island-ness."

God, help me to reflect on some of the temporary friendships in my life and to thank you for them.

⋯⋯⋯⋯⋯⟨ ✳ ⟩⋯⋯⋯⋯⋯

[49] **Mary pondered**

The gospels tell us that Mary liked to ponder things. When the angel Gabriel first appeared to her he said, "Greetings, favored one! The Lord is with you" (Lk 1:28). Mary was "much perplexed by his words and pondered what sort of greeting this might be" (Lk 1:29). Later, when the shepherds came to visit the newborn child, Mary is shown pondering once again: "She treasured all these words and pondered them in her heart" (Lk 2:19).

Twelve years later, when Mary and Joseph found the lost Jesus in the temple, Luke says, "His mother treasured all these things in her heart" (Lk 2:51). She reflected on this event and her son's words to her. Years later on Calvary, John tells us that

Mary was there, "standing near the cross" (Jn 19:25). Even as Jesus was dying, Mary continued to ponder the meaning of this seemingly catastrophic event.

Like Mary, we are called to be ponderers too. We are called to reflect on the events of our lives, to weigh matters carefully before acting, to actively seek new meanings and new possibilities. Sometimes we will ponder in joy—for example, when we see a newborn baby, experience the support of a friend, or receive a consolation in prayer. At other times, we will ponder in sorrow—when we mourn the death of a loved one, behold all the evil in the world, or experience dryness in prayer.

For all of these times, Mary can be our model, for when it comes to pondering, she shows us the way.

*Mary, teach me to ponder the events in my life,
that I may see in them new meanings and new possibilities.*

---

[50] Playing hide-and-seek with a squirrel

Yesterday I saw a squirrel out by the cemetery. As soon as he spotted me, he ran up a tree, stopping about five feet off the ground. Curious, I walked closer to that tree. As I did, the squirrel scooted around to the opposite side of the tree. Then I started to walk slowly around the tree. As I did, the squirrel went around the tree too, always keeping the tree between himself and me. I felt as if I were playing hide-and-seek with him. Just as I was determined to see that squirrel, so was he determined not to be seen by me!

Finally, I stopped and started going in the opposite direction. Sure enough, I caught the squirrel coming around the other way. When he spotted me, he flicked his tail and immediately reversed his direction. Around and around we went again for several more minutes.

Later, I thought: that's how I am with God at times. I'm like that little squirrel, living a life of caution and scurrying. Out of nowhere, God enters my world. I'm afraid (understandably so!), but curious enough (fortunately!) not to run completely away from God. Instead, I scurry up a nearby tree and cling to its solid trunk. When God comes closer, I begin to go around and around the tree, always careful to keep the tree—or some other barrier—between God and me. It's not that I'm terrified of God, mind you. If so, I'd run all the way up to the top of the tree. No, I'm fascinated by God, but also mistrustful enough not to let God get too close.

God, help me to name the barriers I keep between
you and myself. And lead me to trust you more.

---

[51] On giving scandal

If there is one thing Jesus was good at, it was giving scandal. He ate with sinners (Mt 9:9–13), cured on the sabbath (Mk 3:1–6), spoke openly with women on the street (Jn 4:1–42), and even allowed a lady of the night to invade his personal space in broad daylight (Lk 7:36–50). The scribes and Pharisees found such behavior scandalous, shocking, and (eventually) intolerable.

There is something about Jesus giving scandal that attracts me. When I read these accounts, I find myself cheering Jesus on. "You show 'em, Jesus!" I say. "Shock the heck out of them!"

Why do I react this way? It's not because I think scandal is, in itself, a good thing. No. Nor do I think Jesus' aim in these instances was solely to give scandal. On the contrary, Jesus' aim in all of these cases was to do the loving thing. His aim was to make God's love incarnate in this particular time and place, with these specific individuals. If doing that gave scandal to others, then so be it.

The old adage says, "Beauty is in the eye of the beholder." So is scandal. If we do not see with the eyes of Jesus, then we will be scandalized by his actions. But if we do see with Jesus' eyes, we will behold the beauty in everything he did.

God, help me to make your love incarnate in my time and place, with the individuals you put into my day. If doing this gives scandal to others, so be it.

---

[52] **"Here I am, God"**

Throughout Scripture we find individuals saying to God, "Here I am." When God calls to Moses from the burning bush, Moses answers, "Here I am" (Ex 3:4). When God summons Samuel in the middle of the night, Samuel responds with "Here I am" (1 Sm 3:4). And when God asks the prophet Isaiah, "Whom shall I send?" Isaiah replies, "Here am I; send me!" (Is 6:8).

Those three little words make a beautiful prayer. Here I am. Not there. Not where I used to be or where I will be someday or where I wish I were. But here. In this place. Amid these specific circumstances. Here I am. Not as I was yesterday or as I will be tomorrow or as I wish I were. But as I am. In this condition, this shape. With these particular thoughts and feelings.

Perhaps all prayer should begin with a simple "Here I am, God." It should begin with the humble acknowledgment and acceptance of where we find ourselves and who we are on this particular day. Only then can we hope to begin to move forward and beyond—with God's grace, of course.

Here I am, God. With your grace, help me to begin
to move beyond where and who I am today.

---

[53] Fallow time

For six years I lived in Detroit. Since my family and religious community were both near Cleveland, I often drove between the two cities. Whenever I did, I was amazed at all the farmland I saw en route, especially in northwestern Ohio. Literally miles and miles of flat fields stretch as far as the eye can see on both sides of the turnpike. In summer these fields were burgeoning with green crops—mostly corn and soybeans, I noticed. But in the fall, after the crops had been harvested, these same fields were brown and bare, plowed up and lying fallow.

Seeing these fallow fields conjured up for me a line from Sue Bender's book *Everyday Sacred*: "We all need a certain amount of fallow time." Fallow. The word is rich and lovely. Strictly speaking, it describes land that has been plowed up but intentionally left unseeded, thus giving the land a chance to rest, to reclaim its nutrients.

We all need a certain amount of fallow time in our lives. We need times of rest and nonproductivity, times to reclaim our nutrients. In these fallow times we step out of our "doer mode" and slip into our "be-er mode." These are times we just stare out windows, watch clouds float by, listen to crickets chirping, play with a child, daydream. In short, we "waste" time.

What happens when we don't have fallow time in our lives? Bender tells us: "There is a deeper intelligence that won't come forth." That "deeper intelligence" is often, I suspect, the low, sweet voice of God whispering in our hearts.

God, help me to reclaim some fallow time
both in my day and in my life.

---

[54] Keep laughing

Laughing is good for us on all levels: physical, psychological, social, and spiritual. If that is true, then sometimes the best thing for our general well-being is a simple joke, like these:

- A pessimist is someone who looks both ways before crossing a one-way street.
- Question: How many paranoids does it take to change a light bulb? Answer: Why do you want to know?
- As I grow older, there are three things I have trouble remembering: faces, names, and...I can't remember what the third thing is.
- Tell me, how did you become so successful? Two words: right decisions. And how did you make right decisions? One word: experience. And how did you get experience? Two words: wrong decisions.
- Archives: where Noah kept his two bees.

Keep me laughing, God.

[55] **Haste makes sense**

Benjamin Franklin said, "Haste makes waste." But Scripture offers another view. It says that sometimes haste makes sense.

Concerning the first Passover meal, God gives these directives to the Israelites, "You shall eat it hurriedly" (Ex 12:11). After all, if our life is in danger, we'd better not dillydally. Throughout the psalms, we find this prayer addressed to God: "Make haste to help me" (Ps 38:22). When it comes to getting help from God, don't we all want immediate results?

After the Annunciation, Mary goes "with haste to a Judean town in the hill country" (Lk 1:39) to visit her cousin Elizabeth. Joy and excitement have a way of propelling us—even over the hills in life. After Jesus' birth, the shepherds go "with haste" (Lk 2:16) to find the newborn king. When our destination is love incarnate, why would we ever drag our feet? Even Jesus himself encouraged haste. When he spots Zacchaeus in that sycamore tree, Jesus calls, "Zacchaeus, hurry and come down; for I must stay at your house today" (Lk 19:5). Zacchaeus scrambles down from that tree, for, if we receive an invitation from Jesus himself, we hustle.

The truth is, of course, we don't have all the time in the world. Therefore, sometimes we must make haste: when we are fleeing danger, asking for God's help, brimming with joy and excitement, seeking love incarnate, and responding to an invitation from Jesus himself. At such times, haste makes sense. The only sense.

God, make haste to help me. And may I also
make haste to help others today.

[56] Jealousy and our intrinsic ache for "the more"

When I find myself jealous of someone else's talents and good fortune, I am embarrassed. I say to myself, "Why should you be jealous when you've received so many blessings—your family, friends, health, talents? Why can't you just be satisfied?"

Be satisfied? That's the word that helped me see jealousy in a more positive light. Yes, jealousy can be an ugly thing when it blinds us to our own gifts, or when it goads us into wishing or inflicting harm upon another. But jealousy can also be a benevolent thing when it reminds us that we will never be completely satisfied here on earth, no matter how gifted or successful we are, no matter how much love we give and receive. We'll always feel this longing for more. In fact, when we're jealous of others, it's usually because we assume they possess "the more" we're missing—more talent, more money, more power, more freedom, more love. And if only we had what they have, we'd never be jealous again. Ha!

For many of us, jealousy keeps popping up every now and then, reminding us of our intrinsic ache for "the more," which ultimately, of course, is God.

God, you alone can satisfy my deepest longings.
Help me to befriend my intrinsic ache for "the more."

---

[57] The prodigality of the pear trees

Today I bit into a fresh, ripe pear and, *presto*! I was instantly transported back in time (over fifty years) and space (over 220 miles) to our small farm in northeastern Ohio, a farm that doesn't even exist anymore. My right brain did the transporting—instantaneously—leaving my poor left brain scrambling to figure out how I had done it. It kept reasoning, "How could we be in Detroit, Michigan, one minute and in Willoughby Hills, Ohio, the next? And how come it's not today anymore but suddenly fifty years ago?"

Only after a few seconds did my left brain figure it out. "I've got it! It was the taste of that pear!" it concluded excitedly. And it was right. For the pear I had bitten into tasted exactly like the pears we used to have on our farm years ago, pears that were strewn all over our yard in late summer. To my recollection, they all came from five pear trees: three small ones on the side of the house and two very tall ones by the end of the driveway. Every year these five trees provided us with an abundance of pears, even though we never actually cultivated those trees or sprayed them. In fact, we all but ignored them all year long— except in the spring when we admired their blossoms, and in the fall when we ate their fruit.

Sometimes in life, we toil long and hard to produce good fruit: a strong marriage, decent kids, an effective ministry. But other times, the fruit just happens with little or no effort on our part. Or as Scripture says, "A good measure, pressed down, shaken together, running over, will be put into your lap" (Lk 6:38). Kerplunk! Just like that!

Biting into that pear today led me to give thanks for all of life's gratuitous fruits.

Thank you, God, for all the fruits you've
given me out of your prodigality.

[58] Ministry: punishment or privilege?

After teaching four years at Notre Dame College in Cleveland, Ohio, I was transferred to Cardinal Gibbons High School in Raleigh, North Carolina. Here I taught religion and English to seniors. I had been at Gibbons only a week or two, when a senior boy asked at the beginning of class, "Sister, is it true that you taught college before coming here?"

"Yes, I did," I said.

What the boy asked next, I will never forget: "Then being sent here to teach us—was that some kind of a punishment?"

I had to smile at his question—in a way. But in another way, I couldn't, for the boy was completely serious. He was assuming that being sent to Gibbons to teach him and his classmates was some kind of a step down for me.

I assured the boy that coming to Raleigh was not a demotion. And teaching him and his classmates was certainly no punishment. "In fact," I said, "being here with you is a privilege." And I meant those words.

We spend our lives doing all kinds of work and ministry: we raise families, administer parishes, teach CCD, volunteer at soup kitchens. What kind of message do we send to the people we serve? Being here with you is a punishment? Or, being here with you is a privilege?

God, help me to communicate this message to the people
I serve: Being here with you is a privilege!

[59] **Experiencing pleasure**

St. John of Damascus (c. 675–c. 749) taught that the primary purpose of sexual intercourse was pleasure. (Upon hearing that, one of my colleagues remarked, "One wonders how this teaching, over the years, got shuffled to the bottom of the deck!")

Sometimes religious people tend to view pleasure, whether sexual or otherwise, with displeasure, if you will, or with mistrust or even antagonism. We are more apt to associate pleasure with sin than with sanctity. And that's unfortunate. For Scripture tells us over and over again that God is someone who experiences pleasure. "The Lord takes pleasure...in those who hope in his steadfast love" (Ps 147:11). "The Lord takes pleasure in his people" (Ps 149:4). Even Jesus himself described a God who was no stranger to pleasure: "It is your Father's good pleasure to give you the kingdom" (Lk 12:32). Jesus himself was labeled a glutton (Mt 11:19), simply because he took pleasure in tasty food and fine wine.

Pleasure, then, is never bad in itself. On the contrary, it is one of the ways we encounter the divine in the everyday. Simple pleasures (the scent of pine, the feel of a kitten's fur, the song of a wren, the taste of a strawberry, the embrace of a loved one) can bring us closer to God. Enjoying them now prepares us for the fullness of God's presence where there will be "pleasures forevermore" (Ps 16:11).

God, come to me in the pleasures of this day.

[60] **"Give this matter the attention it deserves"**

When Rome sends a letter to the bishops of the world, it often concludes with "Give this matter the attention it deserves." Rome is assuming, I imagine, that all of its matters are of great importance and deserving of serious attention. But I suspect on more than one occasion, there's a bishop somewhere who judges otherwise. "Give this matter the attention it deserves?" he says to himself. "Okay," and he slips the letter underneath the stack of other letters already piled on his desk.

The directive "Give this matter the attention it deserves" has become something of a watchword for me. When some petty thing begins to bother me, I say to myself, "Give this matter the attention it deserves." Translation? "Forget it! It doesn't deserve the attention you're giving it!" Or when some inconsequential task begins to usurp too much of my valuable time and energy, I remind myself, "Give this matter the attention it deserves." In other words, "Let go of it already! It's not worth it!"

Sometimes the opposite happens, and I want to rush through an important job. I remind myself, "Slow down! Give this task the attention it deserves." I have no time to visit a friend or play with a child? I tell myself, "Stop and give them the attention they deserve!"

A grace to pray for: to be able to give all things the attention they truly deserve.

God, help me to give things the attention they deserve today.

[61] **Humility and the illusion of personal autonomy**

In his book *Cherish Christ Above All*, Demetrius Dumm, OSB, says this about humility: "To be humble is to be realistic about what one can or cannot achieve by personal effort. It is opposed, not to self-esteem, but to the illusion of personal autonomy."

Too often in the past we have thought of humility in terms of self-abasement: "I'm nobody...I can't do anything...I'm no good." How much more accurate it is to view humility in terms of our intrinsic need for others: "I can't go it alone...I have to have help with this...I need God."

"The illusion of personal autonomy...." Maybe that's the form pride often takes in our day. Pride: when we deify control and autonomy. Pride: when we assume that our achievements are the sole result of our personal effort. Pride: when we reject the assistance of friend, ally, community, and even God.

God, enable me to be realistic about what I can or cannot achieve by personal effort. In other words, keep me humble.

---

[62] **Putting the groceries away**

There are essentially two attitudes toward putting the groceries away: attitude A and attitude B.

A: These bags weigh a ton. I hate carrying groceries into the house.

B: *How lucky I am to have all these bags of groceries to carry into my house.*

A: Humpf! Bananas went up three cents a pound!

B: *Thank you, God, for giving me bananas in November—and oranges, and apples, and lettuce, too.*

A: I hate this freezer! It's so small, I can hardly fit these frozen vegetables in!

B: *How lucky am I to own a freezer when most of the world's peoples have never even seen one, let alone own one!*

A: That stupid store was out of butter pecan frozen yogurt, so I had to settle for pralines and cream.

B: *I'm amazed at the variety of flavors we have in frozen yogurt these days! With so many, it's hard to decide which one to buy.*

A: I can't believe I was charged for four cans of soup when I bought only three! What an injustice!

B: *So the store charged me for a can of soup I didn't buy. I'll call it to their attention next week—probably. What kind of an injustice is that compared to the kind that deprives millions of people of all food—including even soup?*

A: There! I'm finally finished putting all those groceries away. I'm glad that job's over with!

B: *There! I'm finished putting all my groceries away. How blessed I am!*

Thank you, God, for all the food I have in my house.
Help me to be mindful of those who have little or no food
in their house—if they have a house.

[63] **God likes spunk**

Scripture tells us that God likes submission. "Submit yourselves therefore to God," St. James tells us (Jas 4:7). "Yield yourselves to God," echoes St. Paul (Rom 6:13). And the prophet Samuel makes clear, "To obey is better than sacrifice" (1 Sm 15:22).

Submit. Yield. Obey. Yes, God likes submission. But does God also like spunk? Does God like pluck? I think so. All we have to do is look at Jesus.

Jesus appreciated submission. He appreciated the submission of a Roman centurion (Lk 7:1–10), of the blind Bartimaeus (Mk 10:46–52), of the repentant woman (Lk 7:36–50). But he also appreciated spunk; he also welcomed pluck.

Take, for instance, the story of the Syrophoenician woman (Mk 7:24–30). She comes to Jesus, bows submissively at his feet, and begs him to cure her daughter who was possessed by a demon. She's a Gentile, a non-Jew. Jesus at first seems to refuse her request. "It is not fair to take the children's food and throw it to the dogs," he says. Despite the apparent insult, the woman persists. With incredible spunk (not to mention creativity) she replies, "Sir, even the dogs under the table eat the children's crumbs." Her clever retort wins Jesus over. He says to her (probably with a grin), "For saying that, you may go—the demon has left your daughter." Submission is appreciated, yes, but spunk is rewarded!

Our prayer doesn't always have to be "Thy will be done, Lord...Whatever you say...You know what's best, God." Sometimes God expects and even appreciates it when we fling God's way a few Nos!, Darns!, Hells!, and even Damn its!

God, give me spunk!

[64] "It's okay to have a crabby day"

In his book *Spiritual Surrender*, Jim Krisher relates how, during the early weeks of his marriage, he was having a bad day. For no apparent reason he was sullen and irritable. At the end of the day, he apologized profusely to his wife for his behavior. She simply smiled and said, "It's okay to have a crabby day."

St. Paul says, "God loves a cheerful giver" (2 Cor 9:7). That's true. But it doesn't mean that God expects us to be a cheerful giver 24 hours a day, 365 days out of the year! God is far too much of a realist to demand that, and far too much of a friend. In fact, God would be the first to say to us, "It's okay to have a crabby day." God would also say: It's okay to get tired…It's okay to be sad…It's okay to doubt…It's okay to let your guard down. In other words, it's okay to be human.

God, my friend, let me hear you say to me today,
"It's okay to be human."

---

[65] The tyranny of personal preference

When I taught high school, sometimes my religion class would have a Mass together, and I would recruit a few kids to plan the liturgy. Inevitably, after looking over the readings for the day, one would ask, "Do we have to use the readings of the day—or can we pick the ones we want?" Almost always, I would answer, "Let's use the readings already chosen for this day." My reply usually elicited a groan or two, and one kid would sometimes say, "But we don't like those readings! Why can't we pick ones we like?"

Fair question. Depending on how much time I had, I would explain to my students that sticking only to Scripture we liked was not wise. If we kept choosing only passages that appealed to us, we were selling ourselves short. Scripture is meant to console us, yes. And it usually does that when we hear our favorite passages—like the parable of the prodigal son, for example. But Scripture is also meant to challenge us and, on occasion, even to disturb us. This is more likely to happen when we read passages we don't like, passages which, given the choice, we would prefer to avoid—for example, the parable of the last judgment.

We live in an age that glorifies personal preference. "Have it your way" could well be the watchword of our times. Parents run up against this all the time. They know there are times they can give in to their children's preferences: "What kind of cake would you like for your birthday?" But parents also know that there are times when they must ignore or even go against the preferences of their children: "No, you can't stay home from school today." "You must eat your vegetables!"

Someone once used the expression "the tyranny of personal preference." It's an apt phrase, for if we allow our personal preferences to govern our lives, we will not be free to move beyond where or who we are. Instead, we will be stuck in our own little world—a world cozy and safe, yes, but a world pale and impoverished.

God, move me beyond my personal preferences today.

Winter

[66] **"The conviction of things not seen"**

A man boarded a plane with his son and his son's friend, both of whom were priests. The man sat in the middle seat, a little apprehensive at the prospect of flying. Detecting his fear before takeoff, the flight attendant reassured him cheerfully, "You've got nothing to worry about, sitting between two priests." The man was skeptical. "What do you think priests are?" he asked. "Propellers?"

Authentic faith asks us to trust in things not seen when we'd naturally prefer something much more visible and concrete. In the letter to the Hebrews we read: "Faith is the assurance of things hoped for, the conviction of things not seen" (Heb 11:1). Faith asks us to believe in things that are very real, but not necessarily always visible. What things? The goodness in people, the power of love, the beauty in the ordinary, the presence of God.

God, strengthen my faith today.
Give me the conviction of things not seen.

---

[67] **Befriending darkness**

When Thomas Edison invented the light bulb, he gave us a marvelous gift. But, as with all gifts, the light bulb has its downside: it has given us a lack of appreciation for, or even a mistrust of, darkness.

Think of it: prior to light bulbs, people spent a great part of their lives in the dark—or nearly dark. Candles, kerosene lamps, and gas lights were precious commodities used sparingly. When it got dark, most people either sat in the dark or went to bed. What a contrast to us who just flick on a light and continue to do whatever we were already doing before it got dark. No longer needing to restrict our activities to daylight hours, we have the "luxury" of working twenty-four hours a day if we choose.

John Staudenmaier, SJ, has written and lectured extensively on both the positive and negative influences of modern technology on humanity. He sometimes invites people to abstain from technology for twenty-four hours. If that's not possible, he encourages people at least to do without light bulbs for a day or so. His purpose? To enable people to appreciate the beauty, power, and mystery of darkness, to help them see darkness not merely as the absence of light, but as a beautiful entity in itself. Some wonderful things occur only in darkness: the sprouting of a seed, the development of an unborn child, the bustle of nocturnal animals and insects. We humans know the beauty of eating by candlelight, sitting around a campfire, praying in an unlit chapel, making love in the darkness.

God loves darkness. In fact, it is precisely in darkness that God spoke to Moses: "Then the people stood at a distance, while Moses drew near to the darkness where God was" (Ex 20:21). At the dedication of the Temple, King Solomon says to the people: "The Lord said he would dwell in thick darkness" (1 Kgs 8:12). And the psalmist says of God: "He made darkness his covering around him" (Ps 18:11).

Maybe we would do well to accept Father Staudenmaier's invitation to do without light bulbs for a day or two. Who knows—we might not only befriend darkness, we might even encounter God.

God, help me to befriend the darkness.

[68] **The silver chalice: a sacred trust**

I was making a three-day retreat at the Jesuit retreat center near Detroit. Before Mass, the celebrant told us we would be using the chalice that, in all likelihood, belonged to the Jesuit priest Jacques Marquette, who ministered to Native Americans in Michigan in the seventeenth century. Then he told us the story of the chalice.

In 1912, Father Dunigan, a diocesan priest, was missioned to Michigan's upper peninsula. One day two elderly Native American men came to his Mass. They sat in the back of the small church and gazed at him attentively. After doing this for several days, the two men stopped the priest after Mass and asked if he belonged to the same church that the blackrobes belonged to many years ago. When he said "Yes," the men said, "Then we have something to give you."

The men led the priest into the woods where they stopped at the foot of a giant tree. One of the men began digging in the ground until he unearthed a wooden box. Inside the decaying box was a chalice—blackened with tarnish, but pure silver. The inscription indicated it was, in all probability, Father Marquette's.

The men told Father Dunigan that many years ago a black-robe served their people. When he had to leave, he entrusted the chalice to their tribe with the directive, "Give this to anoth-er blackrobe someday." For 250 years the Native American tribe had carefully guarded this treasure, passing on the secret of its hiding place from one generation to the next. When Father Dunigan appeared, the men felt it was time to hand over the chalice to this new blackrobe.

Dunigan described how he felt when the men placed the chalice into his hands: "Overcome with emotion, holding the sacred cup in trembling hands, I made a little speech of accep-tance to the Indians, and thanked them in the name of Holy

Mother the Church for so nobly acquitting themselves of so sacred a trust."

As I drank from that chalice at Mass that day, I too was filled with emotion as I held the sacred cup in trembling hands.

The story of Father Marquette's chalice is, in miniature, the story of our Christian faith. For our faith, too, is a treasure of incomparable worth passed down from one generation to the next, a treasure with which we are now entrusted.

God, I thank you for all my ancestors in the faith.
May I, like them, prove a worthy custodian
of so valuable a treasure.

---

[69] The inner child

When I was a little girl, I felt sorry for grown-ups. At our family get-togethers, we kids had fun playing hide-and-seek in the corn field or swinging from trees in the backyard, while all the grown-ups did was sit around on lawn chairs and talk. Just talk! At age five, I couldn't imagine anything more boring, more "unfun."

We read much today about getting in touch with our "inner child." That can be a good thing. Jesus himself said, "Unless you change and become like children, you will never enter the kingdom of heaven" (Mt 18:3). It might serve us well, then, to get in touch not only with our own inner child, but also with the inner child of those around us—to view others not as complicated, conniving, and completed adults, but as goodwilled, guileless, and growing children. Trusting that everyone does, indeed, possess an inner child could do wonders for improving relationships.

Jesus, help me to be in touch with my own inner child and the inner child of the individuals you put into my life today.

---

[70] **Look again**

All artists invite us to look again. The poet William Wordsworth invites us to look again at that host of yellow daffodils bobbing in the breeze. The sculptor Michelangelo asks us, "Do you really think you understand the meaning of the crucifixion? Well, look again!" and he places before us his magnificent Pietà for our contemplation. The painter Georgia O'Keeffe says, "You think a red poppy is only a red poppy? Then look again—at mine!"

Jesus, too, invites us to look again. He calls us to look again at our supposed enemy and see a man filled with compassion (Lk 10:25–37). He invites us to look again at an apparently worthless woman and see instead a lady of immense love (Mk 14:3–9). He dares us to gaze upon bread and wine and behold his body and blood (Lk 22:17–20). And he challenges us to look again at suffering and death and to detect in them joy and new life.

Writer John Stewart Collis wrote, "Faith is reborn whenever anyone chooses to take a good look at anything—even a potato." At what individuals or circumstances in my life might Jesus be inviting me to look again?

Jesus, teach me to look again.

[71] Gesture as prayer

Throughout the ages, spiritual writers have maintained that posture and gesture are important components of prayer. Kneeling, for example, is a traditional posture of submission and can call to mind God's sovereignty. Genuflecting and bowing are gestures of reverence and can make us more aware of God's majesty. Closing our eyes can help us to focus better during prayer, while sitting quietly with opened hands on our lap can encourage our receptivity to God's word.

Bodily gestures do more, however, than merely aid us in prayer. Sometimes they themselves actually become our prayer. Rabbi Abraham Heschel said, "When I marched with Martin Luther King in Selma, I felt my legs were praying." How insightful! Ordinary physical movement becoming prayer! In a way, then, our body prays every time it is engaged in loving acts. What kinds of acts? Here are but a few:

Cooking a meal...shoveling snow...pouring coffee at a soup kitchen...addressing Christmas cards...filling a bird feeder...rocking a cranky baby...watering plants...making love with one's spouse...offering an arm to an elderly friend...giving someone a back rub.

God, may I become more aware of my body praying today.

---

[72] Befriending the older and the younger

One study reported that good friends are usually in the same age bracket, that is, within eight years of each other. It's easy to see why. We start off in life doing many things according to age—like going to school. Even after school many of us still gravitate toward people who share a common history with us: "You remember the Brady Bunch too? So do I!"

But our life is impoverished if we befriend only individuals around our age. For individuals both older and younger than we are have a wealth of history and experience to add to our own. I have always admired the friendship of Teresa of Avila and John of the Cross, two great saints of the church. I remember how surprised I was, however, when I learned that Teresa was twenty-seven years older than John.

Surely, one of the best ways to enrich our life is to befriend someone significantly older or younger than ourselves.

God, help me to befriend someone outside my age bracket.

---

[73] "Come, Lord Jesus!"

Advent is the season for longing. The refrain used throughout Advent expresses the essence of our longing: "Come, Lord Jesus!" (Rv 22:20). We long for Jesus to come into our personal lives—our families, parishes, workplaces—into our local communities, and finally, into our nation and world.

With today's media, we are only too aware of those places where Jesus seems to be absent. Perhaps we ourselves are struggling with our own compulsions or are at odds with someone in our family. Or maybe we realize that the poor in our midst are being overlooked by our parish or local community. In addition, we get daily reports of violence and injustices in places all over the globe, places too numerous, unfortunately, to keep track of. This painful awareness of Jesus' apparent absence can serve to intensify our longing for his coming.

Little wonder, then, that the season of Advent appeals to so many people. Its underlying refrain, "Come, Lord Jesus!" is the fundamental cry of our restless and anxious hearts.

Come, Lord Jesus!

---

[74] The Song of Songs

When I was a novice, I remember reading the Song of Songs and blushing. All that stuff about lips, breasts, navels, and thighs made me wonder, "How did this book ever get into the Bible?!" I don't know how the Song of Songs ever made it into the Bible (I do know there was considerable controversy surrounding its inclusion). But I know one thing for sure now: I'm glad it's in!

Why? For one thing, the book is a magnificent celebration of the beauty of sexual love. And anyone who knows the history of the church knows it could use a little celebrating of erotic love. But I like the Song of Songs for yet another reason. It proclaims, in unforgettably beautiful and explicitly sensual language, that God longs for us. Just think of it: God longs for us. The Song of Songs makes clear what type of longing we're talking about, too. It's not the type of longing that has God saying, "I kinda like you." (Here insert a hearty handshake.) No, it's the kind of longing that a lover has for a "lovee." The kind that has God saying, "I desire you! I yearn for you! I want you! Come here!" (And here insert a lover's embrace.)

We are sometimes perceptive enough to realize our longing for God. But how often are we cognizant of God's passionate longing for us? Some lines from the Song of Songs might help us to contemplate this amazing reality. Imagine God saying these words to you:

"Let me see your face, let me hear your voice....Ah, you are beautiful, my love! Truly lovely! How sweet is your love! How much better is your love than wine! Come, my beloved! Let us go forth into the fields....There I will give you my love!"

God, help me to feel your longing for me today.

---

[75] Button up your overcoat

There's an old song entitled "Button Up Your Overcoat." A line in that song that really speaks to me is this: "Take good care of yourself, you belong to me." The line expresses a fundamental truth about value and worth. Sometimes things are valuable simply because of the person to whom they belong. An extreme example: some people go through the *garbage* of famous people looking for items they might sell: coffee grounds, empty milk cartons, and the like. Ridiculous!

More worthy examples would be these: our grandmother's necklace, our father's high school ring, the quilt made by our great-aunt Tilly. These items might not be worth much on the open market, but because of the person to whom they belonged, they are priceless in our eyes.

When I was teaching, I sometimes struggled with seeing the worth of some students—especially when they were unusually ornery. That's one reason I looked forward to meeting their parents or guardians—the people they belonged to. Such encounters often made me appreciate just how valuable each student was. I'd say to myself, "Remember: Jason is Jack and

Karen's son," or "Olivia is Ethel's granddaughter." And if that didn't work for me, then I always fell back onto this solid truth: everyone is of value because everyone belongs to God.

God, help me to believe I belong to you—
and so does everyone else I meet today.

---

[76] The need to please

There was a period in my life when most of my energy went into trying to please everybody. It was as if I had reduced all Ten Commandments to one: "Thou shalt not displease thy neighbor." Several factors brought me to this point in my life.

First of all, I'm a woman. And even though recent years have seen significant strides in raising little girls and little boys with greater equality, most little girls of my generation were largely programmed to be "sugar and spice," that is, to be pleasing and nice. We were taught to be polite, sensitive, submissive, caring.

And if being a woman wasn't enough, I eventually became a nun—and everyone knows nuns were expected to be pleasing and nice all the time. We were supposed to please everyone— our sisters, superiors, students, pastors, and (of course) God. If we ever slipped up and displeased or hurt anyone, we were taught to ask for a penance.

Trying to please everybody is a terrible way to live, for to achieve such a goal is downright impossible. By saying this, I am not advocating insensitivity to others. What I am saying is this: 1) Just because someone is hurt or displeased by what I say or do does not mean I am guilty of something. Sometimes I will hurt or displease others simply by being who I am, by making perfectly good and valid choices, and by speaking the truth that needs to be spoken. And 2) if I do hurt or displease someone and I rightly feel some guilt for what I've said or done, then Jesus advocated a wonderful energy-saving device to use in such instances: just say, "I'm sorry."

God, free me from my need to please everybody.
And help me know when to say "I'm sorry."

———————————— ⟨※⟩ ————————————

[77] Humorous observations

Admiration is our polite recognition of another's resemblance to ourselves. ❋ Anonymous

Why is it that a twenty-dollar bill looks so large in the collection basket in church and so small in the grocery store? ❋ Anonymous

Someone suggested this reponse to "Have a nice day": "Thank you, but I have other plans." ❋ Paul Fussell

A successful politician is someone who can stand on a fence and make people believe it's a platform. ❋ Anonymous

When St. John Bosco was dying, he was asked what his two favorite books were. He said, "My Bible and my joke book."

Keep me laughing, God.

[78] Criticism: speaking the truth in love

Someone once asked a bishop who his spiritual advisor was. The bishop replied, "Just about everyone in the diocese!" The truth is, most of us will never lack for advisors or critics. All we have to do is say or do something, and they are sure to appear.

For some of us, criticism is hard to accept. Franklin Jones probably summed up how many of us feel about criticism: "Honest criticism is hard to take, particularly from a relative, a friend, an acquaintance, or a stranger."

Some of us get very defensive about criticism, saying with Benjamin Disraeli, "It is much easier to be critical than correct." Or we side with Kenneth Tynan who said, "A critic is someone who knows the way, but can't drive the car."

But in our better moments we realize that constructive criticism can be very helpful. Norman Vincent Peale once said, "The trouble with most of us is that we would rather be ruined by praise than saved by criticism." How would I define criticism? Relying on St. Paul, I'd say criticism is "speaking the truth in love" (Eph 4:15). But when we do this, we must humbly remember: we are speaking the truth as we see it. And none of us has a monopoly on truth.

Mother Janet Stuart, a nineteenth-century English nun, wrote, "To accept criticism is one of the greatest lessons to be learned in life." I would add, so is learning to give criticism honestly and humbly.

God, teach me to accept and give criticism more graciously.

[79] **Inviting God to take over**

I was telling a friend about a difficult situation I was caught up in. I described the misunderstanding, the confusion, and the pain, hoping to solicit from him a possible solution to my problem or, at least, some well-deserved sympathy.

In one way, he gave me neither. But in another way, he gave me both. For my friend didn't say, "I'll tell you what to do, Melannie!" nor "You poor thing! What a terrible mess you're in!" Instead, he said, "Well, Melannie, that sounds like a good situation for God to get involved in—and maybe even take over."

My friend's response was exactly what I needed to hear. And I realized that the only way God was going to get involved in my messy situation was if I let God get involved. And how was I going to do that? First, by sharing with God everything I had shared with my friend: all the thoughts and feelings, the hurt and anger, the worries and dread—everything. Next, I had to invite God to enter my situation, and I had to ask God to take over.

I had gone to my friend seeking a solution and some sympathy. But he placed before me something far greater: the blazing truth of God's intimate involvement in my personal life, even during the messy times.

God, please come into my life today and take over.

---

[80] **Working and loafing**

The priest asked the kindergartners, "What's your favorite story about Jesus?" One little boy responded instantly: "The story where Jesus loafs and fishes!"

That little boy is on to something. When we adults read the

gospels, we tend to see a very busy Jesus (much like ourselves)—a Jesus preaching, teaching, traveling, healing, and feeding the multitudes. But do we ever see Jesus loafing? Are we able to picture him resting against a tree and dangling a fishing line into a river?

Such an image is not too far-fetched really. John's gospel tells us that Jesus took time to attend a wedding (Jn 2:1–11). And by all accounts, he was leisurely enjoying himself there and had no intention of working that day—that is, not until his mother noticed the wine was running out. The gospels also show us Jesus taking time to dine with friends—Simon the leper (Mk 14:3), Zacchaeus (Lk 19:5–10), and Mary and Martha (Lk 10:38–42). He was so relaxed once that he fell asleep in a boat, perfectly content to entrust the chores of sailing to his friends, until the storm grew too fierce for even their experienced hands (Mt 8:23–27). And how did Jesus ever come up with such great stories (the prodigal son, the good Samaritan) and with such vibrant images (the mustard seed, old and new wineskins, bread rising) unless he made time to stop, listen, observe, and "recollect in tranquility" all he was experiencing?

Jesus works, yes. The gospels make that clear. But the little kindergartner is right. Jesus also loafs and fishes.

Jesus, help me to balance all my working with loafing.

---

[81] Emmanuel

The word "Emmanuel" is an Advent/Christmas word first spoken by the prophet Isaiah to King Ahaz. "Look," he says to the king, "the young woman is with child and shall bear a son, and shall name him Emmanuel" (Is 7:14). It is the same name the angel speaks to a distressed Joseph who has just learned that his fiancée is pregnant—and not by him. "Look," says the angel, "the virgin shall conceive and bear a son, and they shall name him Emmanuel" (Mt 1:23). Then the angel adds, "Which means, 'God is with us.'"

Emmanuel. The word invites reflection. God is with us. *Is* with us. Not just was with us—somewhere back then. Not just will be with us—somewhere in the future. But is with us. Here and now. Do we really believe this? If we do, that belief will color the way we look at everything—from ants to oceans, from people to planets, from pain to ecstasy. It will make us realize, this world can't be that bad a place—not if God is here in it too! My personal life can't be that bad either, that insignificant—not if God is with me!

But I had one Scripture professor who gave me an additional insight into the word "Emmanuel." He said, "The word 'Emmanuel' means more than 'God is with us.' It means 'God is *for* us.'"

God is for us. God is "pro me." This means that God is not some disinterested bystander in my life. God is on my side, in my corner, actively pulling for me all the way.

God, Emmanuel, help me to realize you are
with and for me today.

---

[82] All was not calm, all was not bright

At Christmas time we sing the beautiful hymn "Silent Night." In it we say, "All is calm, all is bright." But if we read the story of the first Christmas, we will conclude, "All was not calm, all was not bright."

All was not calm. When Gabriel first appears to Mary, she is "very much perplexed by his words" (Lk 1:29). When Joseph learns that Mary is pregnant, he too is deeply disturbed (Mt 1:18–20). A terribly inconvenient journey from Nazareth to Bethlehem immediately precedes the birth of Jesus. And shortly after that, Joseph's "dream angel" reappears and warns him to pack up his family and hightail it to Egypt. Where's the calm in all of that?

All was not bright. The Christmas story reminds us that sometimes all is not bright; rather, all is darkness, uncertainty, and confusion. Mary's "yes" at the Annunciation was a "yes" of faith—not certainty. She knew very little, if anything, of what lay ahead for her. As we have seen, Joseph too walked not in clarity but in a cloud, being forced to wait for God to direct his next move.

The lessons of the Christmas story are clear. We must never expect our lives to be calm just because we are trying to be good people. Sometimes God's presence in our lives, like in the lives of Mary and Joseph, will be accompanied by serious disturbances. Similarly, we will not always see clearly what to do next. But Christmas reminds us we walk not always in brightness, but always by faith.

God, when my life is not calm and bright,
help me to walk by faith.

---

[83] God works through all kinds of people

The story of the first Christmas sets before us a marvelous array of individuals: a teenage mother, a conscientious young carpenter, an egotistical emperor, a bevy of angels, a band of hardworking shepherds, a trio of scholarly star gazers, a wise old holy man, an elderly prophetess, and a megalomaniacal king. And, lest we forget, a baby!

A lesson we learn from the story of the first Christmas is this: God works through all kinds of people. All kinds: the young and the old, the simple and the sophisticated, the rich and the poor, the good and the bad. Incredibly, each of the individuals played a role in salvation history. Some did this knowingly, others without a clue. Some did this through their love and goodness, others through their hatred and evil. The amazing thing is that God can use everyone to effect salvation—even me. The only question is this: what kind of a role will I choose to play?

In Romans we read, "We know that all things work together for good for those who love God" (Rom 8:28). Isn't that some of the best news in the entire Good News?

God, work through me today in some small way!

---

[84] **Enlarging our borders**

The Israelites were very concerned with borders. In the book of Exodus, for example, God says to Moses, "I will cast out nations before you and enlarge your borders" (Ex 34:24). We can almost hear the people yelling, "Yippee! Less land for our enemies! More land for us!" This preoccupation with territorial borders is found in Deuteronomy too: "When the Lord your God enlarges your territory as he promised you..." (Dt 12:20). Even the psalms speak of borders: "(God) grants peace within your borders" (Ps 147:14). (As a young nun, I lived in a boarding school with fifty-six teenage boarders, and I often prayed fervently, "God, grant peace within our boarders!")

But what if we think of "borders" not as geographic demarcations, but rather as limits to our own selves? Our borders: "Here is where I end and you begin. This is the extent of my knowledge. These are the perimeters of my love." If we think of borders in these terms, then God's promise, "I will enlarge your borders," takes on new meaning. It means that God will help us to live beyond where we are now, to extend our knowledge, to deepen our understanding, to widen the sweep of our love.

It is not always easy for us to enlarge our lives. We have this natural tendency to want carefully delineated borders, clearly established lines. It's safer that way. Neater too. But God is always urging us toward "the more." "Grow...expand...stretch... move beyond," God says to us. And sometimes (sadly) we refuse, saying, "I don't wanna!" But sometimes (happily) we say "yes" to God's invitation—even though we may, in the process, cry, "Ouch!"

God, enlarge my borders!

---

[85] **Fear is a funny thing**

As his parents go to turn off the light in his bedroom at night, Dennis the Menace begs them, "Please leave the light on!" They reassure him, "You don't have to be afraid of the dark." To which Dennis replies, "I'm not afraid of the dark. I'm afraid of what's *in* the dark!"

Fear is a funny thing. Maybe the adjective "funny" isn't

exactly appropriate, for fear is a very serious thing. In fact, fear is the underlying cause of many of our most serious problems. Thomas Merton said that fear was at the root of all war. The eighteenth-century writer Giambattista Casti would agree, for he wrote, "Short is the road that leads from fear to hate." And author Jim Wallis summed it all up when he said, "Our most deadly enemy is fear."

Yet fear isn't always our deadly enemy. Sometimes it can be our friend. A student of mine admitted to her psychologist one day that she had seriously considered suicide. "But I was too afraid to go through with it," she said, almost apologetically. Her psychologist replied, "Sometimes being afraid is a very good thing."

When, then, is fear our enemy, and when is it our friend? It is our enemy if it breeds mistrust, greed, hatred, violence, and the like. But it is our friend if it reminds us of the precariousness of human existence, the fragility of relationships, and the very real limits of time and resources. Fear is good if it leads us to take care of, nourish, use wisely, and appreciate.

John Macmurray said that all religions are ultimately concerned with overcoming fear. But he distinguished between what he called illusory religion and real religion. Illusory religion says, "Fear not; trust in God and God will see that none of the things you fear will happen to you." Real religion, on the contrary, says, "Fear not; the things you fear may happen to you, but they are really nothing to be afraid of." In other words, darkness in life is very real. But God is in the darkness with us. Or, as the psalmist says to God, "Darkness is not dark to you; the night is as bright as the day" (Ps 139:12).

Jesus knew this. He experienced it through his passion, death, and resurrection. Little wonder, then, he says to us with such conviction, "Fear not, little flock!" (Lk 12:32).

God, you are with me in my darkness.
Let me hear you say to me, "Fear not!"

---

[86] New Year's resolutions

Most of us are good at making New Year's resolutions. "I will lose twenty pounds...I will exercise every day...I will spend more time with my family...I will go to Mass more often..." Making resolutions is easy. It's keeping them that's difficult.

That realization led me to wonder what Scripture says about making resolutions. The Bible is filled with people making resolutions and then breaking them. At the time of the Exodus, Pharaoh resolves to let the Hebrews go (he had been plagued enough!). But as soon as the people start to pull out en masse, Pharaoh breaks his resolution and charges after them with his army (Ex 14). In the gospels, Peter vows at the Last Supper never to desert Jesus (Mt 26:35), but shortly afterwards he denies even knowing Jesus when challenged by a servant girl around a camp fire (Mt 26:69–75). These examples (and many others in Scripture) only prove: 1) how hard it is to keep a resolution, and 2) how true to life the Bible is.

But the Bible also sets before us individuals who made resolutions and kept them. God, for example! After destroying the earth with that terrible deluge, God resolves never to do that again. He promises Noah, "I will never again curse the ground because of humankind" (Gn 8:21). That's one resolution God has kept—at least according to the last time I looked out my window. But, more importantly, God's biggest resolve is the covenant God establishes with Israel; a covenant built on God's promise, "I will not forget you" (Is 49:15–16).

Jesus himself makes and keeps some pretty important resolutions. To those burly fisherman on the shore he says, "Follow me, and I will make you fish for people" (Mk 1:17). Later he shares with his apostles his resolve to go to Jerusalem where he will be tortured and killed. When Peter tries to dissuade him from keeping this resolution, Jesus calls him "Satan" and a "stumbling block to me!" (Mt 16:21–23). And finally, Jesus promises his apostles that, after being dead for three days, he will rise again (Lk 9:22). Our entire Christian faith rests on the belief that Jesus kept this resolution.

> *God, help me to make good resolutions and,*
> *with your help, to keep them.*

---

[87] On being perfect

One of Jesus' sayings that has caused consternation for many is this: "Be perfect, therefore, as your heavenly Father is perfect" (Mt 5:48). I know some individuals who have agonized over that word "perfect." One elderly sister, frustrated by her faults, cried to me, "But Jesus told us to be perfect!"

"Not exactly," I said. To begin with, only Matthew uses the word "perfect" here. The Lucan parallel uses the word "merciful" (Lk 6:36). Big difference. In English, the word "perfect" means flawless. And no human being can lay claim to being that—not even the saints. The word merciful doesn't imply perfection.

Another way of looking at this saying of Jesus came to me from a Scripture professor. She said, "Think of the word 'perfect' as meaning complete." When we strive for perfection, she explained, what we are really striving for is completion, that is, for wholeness. That interpretation also makes more sense to me.

The question we should ask ourselves, then, is not, "How perfect am I?" But "How merciful am I? How far have I progressed toward wholeness?"

Jesus, make me merciful and whole
as your heavenly Father is merciful and whole.

---

[88] St. Valentine's Day

One of my favorite days of the year is Valentine's Day. It ranks almost as high as Christmas and Thanksgiving for me. Why this fondness for a day that, some would say, is promoted solely to sell cards, flowers, and candy? Because Valentine's Day reminds us how precious love is.

And to think all love started with God! At least that's what St. John tells us: "We love, because God first loved us" (1 Jn 4:19). That's why on Valentine's Day I naturally think of God, the greatest lover of them all. And, like all lovers, God shows the symptoms of someone in love, namely, blindness and foolishness.

God is blind. How else can we explain the fact that humankind has somehow endured all these centuries despite our pettiness, greed, laziness, dishonesty, wars, violence, cruelty, and all the other evils too numerous and too depressing to list? As one ten-year-old boy said, after becoming more aware of just a few of the injustices in the world, "If I was God, I would've zapped human beings a long time ago!"

But the truth is God has not zapped us. Obviously, then, God is blind—or at least God sees things differently than we do. Didn't God say as much through the prophet Isaiah? "My thoughts are not your thoughts, nor are your ways my ways" (Is 55:8). Translation: "My way of seeing and doing things is not your way."

Like any lover, God does foolish things in the name of love. One foolish thing God did was to give us free will, thus opening the door to sin. But the gift of free will also opened the door to love. With infinite wisdom, God must have weighed all things in a balance and opted for love. How crucial love must be!

Which is exactly what Valentine's Day celebrates. It calls us to celebrate the love we experience from family and friends. And it reminds us to give thanks to the source of that love, God, the greatest lover of them all!

God, thank you for the gift of love.

---

[89] I yawned at Mass today

...right at the consecration. A big yawn, too. Just as the priest was pronouncing the words, "This is my body...This is my blood." As soon as I realized it, I covered my mouth, of course. But I was aware of what I had done. Priest: "This is my body..." Me: "HO-HUM!"

Afterward I asked myself. "How could you yawn during the consecration of the Mass—during one of the most sacred events in the universe?" My answer: "I don't always measure up to my beliefs."

None of us completely measures up to the things we profess to believe in. We pray, "Thy will be done," and yet we balk every time God's will causes us the least inconvenience. We proclaim "universal charity," and yet we cling to our prejudices. We say prayer means a lot to us, but, given the choice, we opt for other things.

The cure for this? It starts with humble awareness—awareness of those times when we do fall short of incarnating our religious beliefs. My yawn at Mass wasn't my first; nor will it be my last. And, seen in perspective, a yawn is small and insignificant compared to some of the other ways we may fall short in our faith. But today my yawn did me a great service, by leading me to see there's often a gap between what I believe and what I do—a gap bridged only by God's mercy.

God, help me to incarnate my religious beliefs better,
and show me mercy when I don't.

---

[90] Homilies

A preacher began his sermon to his new congregation with these words: "As I see it, my job is to talk to you; your job is to listen. If you finish your job before I finish mine, just raise your hand."

The sermon or homily is one of the most important parts of the Mass, for that's where the preacher takes the readings of the day and applies them to the here and now, to this specific congregation. And that's vital. Otherwise, we may be tempted to think of the readings as a message for an earlier age or for "those other people over there." Because the Scripture readings are so old, we can sometimes think of them as a family heirloom—our great-great-grandmother's china tea set, for example—something we cherish but would never think of actually using.

But a good homily won't allow us to do that. It won't let us get away with saying things like this: "How dense those apostles were!" "Look at how blind those Pharisees are!" "Why don't those Corinthians pay more attention to St. Paul's words?" No, a good homily will make us say things like this: "Sometimes I'm as dense as those apostles." "What am I blind to in my life?" "How can we put into practice today what St. Paul is telling us?"

God, continue to speak to me through Scripture and homilies.

⟨ ❋ ⟩

[91] **The school crossing guard**

I was driving by the Catholic church at 2:30 in the afternoon. It was the week before Christmas, and it was pouring rain. As I waited for the light to change, I spotted her: the school cross-ing guard. She was wearing big boots, jeans, a bright orange vest, and a yellow rain cap. And she was holding in her hand a big red STOP sign. But here's the fun part! She was standing *inside* the life-size Christmas crèche in front of the church! Yes, there she was, standing next to St. Joseph—who didn't seem to mind at all her being there! Apparently, while waiting for the dismissal bell to ring, the woman had used her common sense and had taken refuge from the rain in the manger.

Seeing her there, I laughed out loud. What a source for meditation! First, it was as if she was telling all passersby to STOP! STOP your racing around for a minute; STOP your frenzied Christmas shopping; STOP your worrying; STOP your complaining about the weather; and remember the real reason for this season: the birth of this little baby boy.

In addition, she was, by her placement, physically demon-strating what many spiritual writers (most notably St. Ignatius of Loyola) encouraged us to do: to place ourselves into the Scripture stories. Here she was, literally putting her whole self directly into that manger! St. Ignatius would have been proud!

And finally, the woman looked perfectly at ease in that manger—as if she belonged there. She looked comfortable and safe, too. But she wouldn't remain in that shelter for very long. For in a few minutes the dismissal bell would ring, the children would come pouring out of the school, and she would begin her work, her ministry, if you will: helping the children cross the street in safety. At Christmas, God calls us into the manger to adore. But then God sends us forth into the world, where, like this school crossing guard, we help others safely home.

Jesus, help me to immerse myself in Scripture.

---

[92] Will the magic happen again today?

Sister Laura Wingert, SND, is an artist and a good friend of mine. A teacher of art for many years, she has won numerous awards and prizes for her artwork—drawings, paintings, sculpture, photography, weavings, and (her specialty) clay pots.

Laura and I have had numerous conversations about the creative process. We both speak of the "terror" that precedes our creating something—she, the terror of the empty canvas or unformed lump of clay, I, the terror of the empty page or blank computer screen. What we are both admitting to is this: the ability to create something—anything—is mostly gift. Realizing this, Laura (every time she sits down to draw) and I (every time I sit down to write) wonder: "Will I be inspired today? Will the magic happen again?"

The magic, of course, is the ability to fashion something that transcends our personal limitations, something that surprises and delights us—the creators—as much as it may surprise and delight our audience or readers. Sure, the magic may have happened yesterday and the day before—and perhaps even a thousand times before. But the question always remains: will the magic happen today?

This doesn't mean that artists don't work hard. We do. Very hard. But deep in our hearts we know that inspiration is something we have little control over. We all rely on something (someone?) beyond ourselves to produce what we do. The ancient Greeks had a name for this thing: the muse, they called it. Laura and I prefer to call it "the creative and holy Spirit."

Holy Spirit, make the magic happen in my life today.

---

[93] Emperor penguins

I once read an article on emperor penguins by Glenn Oeland in *National Geographic* magazine. Of all penguins, emperors are the only ones that stay in Antarctica during the winter. Amazingly, some 400,000 of them actually breed in winter—in temperatures of forty degrees below zero! Says Oeland, "The simple fact that they succeed (in breeding) is a source of wonderment."

After the usual two-week courtship, the female lays a single egg the size of a softball. Then she goes on a two-month feeding spree, leaving her husband at home to incubate the egg, "with only his body fat to sustain him." The male keeps the egg on top of his feet for sixty-five days. He does nothing else during this time but stand and incubate. Little wonder he loses up to half his body fat in the process. When the chick finally hatches, it spends the first two months in either of its parents' brood pouch. If the chick should tumble from that haven, it can freeze to death in less than two minutes.

As naturalist Graham Robertson puts it, "Emperors live on the cutting edge of life itself." They manage to survive for chiefly two reasons. First, they possess an extremely dense plumage—eighty feathers per square inch. Secondly, during blizzards, they forget all about their individual territories and coalesce into a single mass. Says Robertson, "Like people in a crisis, they forget their differences and rally together."

And so again, another member of the animal kingdom can inspire us human beings. "Wear thick feathers," these penguins tell us (or thick skin, if you prefer). "And during the blizzards of life, forget about retaining your territory and rally together."

God, give me thick plumage to withstand life's bitter winds.
And let me not wait for a crisis to rally together with others.

———————⋖ ⁂ ⋗———————

[94] **Remember to remember**
One of the most frequently used words in Scripture is the word "remember." In the Hebrew Scriptures, we are told over and over again that God is someone who remembers: "And God remembered Noah (Gn 8:1)...God remembered Abraham (Gn 19:29)...God remembered Rachel (Gn 30:22)...God remembered his covenant" (Ex 2:24).

Over and over again in Scripture God reminds people to remember: "Remember the Sabbath day (Ex 20:8)...Remember my covenant with Jacob (Lv 26:42)...Remember all the commandments" (Nm 15:39). The psalms, too, are often prayers asking God to remember: "Be mindful of your mercy" (Ps 25:6); or to forget: "Do not remember the sins of my youth" (Ps 25:7).

The New Testament also shows how important remembering is. Only one-tenth of the lepers remembered to come back and thank Jesus for being cured. Jesus obviously appreciates the fact that at least one of them remembered to say "thanks" (Lk 17:11–19). Several times Jesus warns his apostles of his passion and death, "so that when their hour comes you may remember that I told you about them" (Jn 16:4). And as Jesus was hanging on the cross, one of the men being executed with him begs, "Jesus, remember me when you come into your kingdom." And Jesus replies, "Truly I tell you, today you will be with me in Paradise" (Lk 23:42–43). In other words, "Don't worry. I'll remember you!"

When I give talks and retreats, I usually tell the people that much of what I am going to say, they already know. My job as speaker or retreat director (or writer) is largely to remind them of things already nestling in their minds and hearts.

Jesus, remember me! And teach me to remember to remember!

⟨⟩⟨⟩

[95] **The good thing about being an addict**

I have several friends who are in A.A. One said to me the other day, "The good thing about being an addict is you know you can never get well without help."

His words surprised me. I had never imagined there was anything good about being an addict, whether you had surrendered yourself to something obviously destructive (like drugs, alcohol, or gambling) or to something less noticeably lethal (like chocolate, computer games, or romance novels) or to something apparently noble (like church ministry!).

In his book *Intimacy with God*, Thomas Keating, a Cistercian monk, makes the claim that we all suffer from some form of addiction. Keating maintains that we must admit our powerlessness to God before we can begin to turn our lives around. Members of A.A. know this. They do it. It only makes sense. If we're stuck in mud up to our knees, it's only natural to yell "HELP!" and allow someone else to help pull us out.

In his second letter to the Corinthians, St. Paul tells of being given "a thorn...a messenger of Satan to torment me" (2 Cor 12: 7). No one knows for sure what that thorn was. But perhaps it was some form of addiction. Whatever it was, Paul begs God three times to take this torment away. But God replies: "My grace is sufficient for you, for power is made perfect in weakness" (2 Cor 12:9).

God, may I acknowledge my addictions and
my weaknesses, and yell for help.

---

[96] Looking for God in unfamiliar places

W. Paul Jones, a professor of ecumenism at a Methodist seminary, offers a fascinating suggestion for furthering ecumenism. He suggests that each of us expose ourselves to contrasting expressions of church. He suggests, for example, that a Quaker enter a cathedral for Christmas midnight Mass, that a Southern Baptist spend time in a Benedictine monastery, that a

Trappist monk participate in an inner-city storefront church speaking in tongues, and that a TV evangelist spend a few hours with a hermit whose motto over the door is that of St. Bernard of Clairvaux: "Love to be unknown." And finally, that a bishop share communion with a handleless cup in an Appalachian shack.

Jones' suggestion has implications that go beyond ecumenism. If followed in other areas of our life, his suggestion could broaden our perspective, deepen our spirituality, and enrich our entire lives. It could lead us to find God in places we haven't looked yet. With this in mind, we might want to do something like this:

Befriend someone very different from ourselves...attend a service in a church very unlike our own...read a book or see a movie we ordinarily wouldn't read or see...listen to music we've never listened to before...pray in a way we've never prayed before.

God, help me to look for you in unfamiliar places.

---

[97] Crossword puzzles

Quick! What's a five-letter word for "gambler"? "Player"? No, that's six letters. "Bettor"? No, that's six, too. Here's a hint: it begins with the letter "D." Give up? It's "dicer"! Okay, here's another one. Give me a five-letter word for the verb "propose." "Urge"? No, that's four letters. I'll give you a hint. It begins with "O." That's right, "offer"!

In case you haven't guessed it, I like crossword puzzles. I love the challenge of finding the correct answers. In each instance, only one word is correct, too. Both "raze" and "ruin" might fit in the squares as synonyms for "devastate," but only one is the right answer—its rightness being determined by whether it fits with the other answers around it.

I used to devise crossword puzzles for my students as a fun way to review key terms before a test. I was amazed at how even sophisticated high school kids liked them. When they finally came up with the correct answer they often let out an audible sigh that was a mixture of delight and relief. Then they'd give me a knowing glance that said, "I got it!"

Life is sometimes like a crossword puzzle. We agonize over the clues it gives us. We often propose a variety of answers as to its meaning. But then comes the day we finally come up with the correct answer. Maybe it's "love" or "faith" or "hope" or "forgiveness." And when we do get the answer, we let out an audible sigh that is a mixture of delight and relief. And we whisper to God, "I got it!"

Quoting Isaiah, John the Baptist announced the coming of God's kingdom with these words: "Every valley shall be filled, and every mountain and hill shall be made low, and the crooked shall be made straight, and the rough ways be made smooth" (Lk 3:5). He could just as easily have added, "And every word will come into the crossword puzzle!"

God, help me to get it.

Spring

[98] The newborn calf

I spot the newborn calf out in the pasture. Pure white, he was born just a few days ago and is now jumping up and down all over the place. As he romps around the pasture, I can almost hear him calling to his mother nearby, "Hey, Ma! Look at what I can do with these legs!" And he kicks his little rear end up in the air a few times to impress her.

His mother, however, is not impressed. In fact, she isn't even paying attention to him. Rather, she is standing motionless and eyeing me with grave suspicion. I can almost hear her warning me, "Don't you dare come any closer to my calf!" The motionless mother cow is a sharp contrast to her frisky little son.

As I watch the two of them, I find myself identifying with the cow. I, too, have been motionless these past several weeks—maybe "stuck" is a better word. I, too, have been eyeing with suspicion everything and everyone around me. I, too, have been silently warning others, "Don't come any closer!" As a result, I feel stodgy, old, and too used to things. I envy the joy and exuberance of the newborn calf, and I pity the jadedness of his mother.

As we graze in the pasture of life, I think we're meant to be more calf than cow. I think God wants us to retain our playful exuberance no matter how old we get, how many responsibilities we bear, how many problems we encounter. We will succeed in doing this, too, only if we remember: Never take anything for granted—legs, the other cows, even the pasture itself. And never forget to entrust our safekeeping to God, our loving Creator.

God, help me to count my blessings joyfully.

[99] **Conversion**

In the Acts of the Apostles we read of the conversion of
St. Paul (Acts 9:1–19). Saul (later called Paul) is on his way
to Damascus to round up some Christians to drag back to
Jerusalem. Suddenly "a light from heaven" flashes around Saul,
hurling him to the ground. Temporarily blinded, he hears the
voice of Jesus asking him, "Saul, Saul, why do you persecute
me?" We know how the story ends. Saul makes a 180-degree
turn in his life, eventually becoming the leading evangelizer in
the early church.

On the surface, it looks as if Paul's conversion was almost
instantaneous. One day seething persecutor, next day ardent
devotee. But if we read an earlier story of the stoning of St.
Stephen, we find this intriguing sentence: "Then they dragged
(Stephen) out of the city and began to stone him; and the wit-
nesses laid their cloaks at the feet of a young man named Saul"
(Acts 7:58). Perhaps Saul's conversion began with the coura-
geous martyrdom of Stephen—or even earlier.

I have always been a little suspicious of "instant conver-
sions." I don't deny they can happen; I just think gradual con-
versions are the norm.

In *Surprised by Joy*, C.S. Lewis describes his own conversion to the faith, a rather lengthy and convoluted one. In
vivid and even humorous terms, he describes the culminating
moment of that conversion, when, alone in his room, he finally
knelt down and admitted that "God was God." Contrasting
himself with the prodigal son, he writes: "The Prodigal Son at
least walked home on his own feet. But who can duly adore
that Love which will open the high gates to a prodigal who is
brought in kicking, struggling, resentful and darting his eyes in
every direction for a chance to escape?" Lewis dubbed himself
fittingly "the most...reluctant convert in all England."

*God, continue to convert me to walk in your ways
—no matter how long it takes.*

<hr />

[100] Offer it up

As children, when our TV went on the blink and we'd complain, my parents would say, "Offer it up." In school, when we couldn't go outside for recess because of the rain, the teachers would say, "Offer it up." And when we didn't eat any candy during Lent, we knew why we were doing it: we were offering it up.

Offer it up—"it" being this disappointment, this pain, this sacrifice. "Offer up" meaning (presumably) to God. In recent years, the phrase "offer it up" has fallen into disfavor. One reason is because the phrase sometimes was a euphemism for "Shut up!": "The Mass is meaningless to me." "Offer it up!" "My husband drinks." "Offer it up!" "I feel called to do more in the church, but I'm a woman." "Offer it up!"

But the phrase continues to express a dynamic that is very integral to our Christian faith. "Offer it up" does not mean we should shut up and suffer or that we should not make changes. It does mean, however, that some things are within our control, and some things are not. And like the so-called "serenity prayer" says, we should pray for the wisdom to know the difference.

Furthermore, "Offer it up" reminds us that we are not in this thing (life!) alone. We are in it together with a host of others—the people next door as well as the people on the other side of the world, those individuals who are already deceased and those who haven't even been born yet. We offer things up for others—that is, we make sacrifices for them—precisely because that's what Jesus did. Jesus laid down his life for us. Translation? He offered himself up for us.

Jesus, help me to offer up my life for others, as you did.

⋖⟨❋⟩⋗

[101] **Wonder: behold!**

Wonder is a holy and powerful thing. According to journalist Bill Moyers, wonder has the power to make people moral. In his book *A World of Ideas II*, Moyers describes watching the launch of Apollo 17. He describes the rocket rising off the launching pad amid brilliant flames and deafening thunder. He tells how a sense of wonder fills everyone as they watch the mighty ship go up and up and up. They gaze in amazement as the first stage ignites a beautiful blue flame. Writes Moyer, the rocket "becomes like a star, but you realize there are humans on it." As the ship soars out of sight, a hush falls over the crowd.

Later, as the people begin to leave, Moyer describes the effect that the launch has had on them: "People just get up quietly, helping each other up. They're kind. They open doors. They look at one another, speaking quietly and interestedly. These were suddenly moral people because the sense of wonder, the experience of wonder, had made them moral."

Perhaps that's why Jesus encouraged us so many times to "behold" things. Behold the lilies of the field...behold the birds of the air...behold the bread rising...behold the wine fermenting. Maybe Jesus, too, believed morality begins with wonder.

Jesus, teach me to "behold" things
so I may become more moral.

[102] "It's all right"

In her book *The Summer of the Great-Grandmother*, Madeleine L'Engle describes in poignant detail how she cared for her elderly mother during her final months. Mentally confused and physically incapacitated, her mother is periodically overcome with fear. One time in particular, the old woman, now confined to her bed, reaches for her daughter and cries, "I'm scared, I'm scared." L'Engle describes what she does:

"I put my arms around her and hold her. I hold her as I held my children when they were small and afraid of the night...I hold her as she, once upon a time and long ago, held me. And I say the same words, the classic, maternal, instinctive words of reassurance: 'Don't be afraid. I'm here. It's all right.'"

L'Engle goes on to say that, even though she does not understand those words, "I mean them." What's more, she says those words of reassurance are behind everything she does—from writing books to cooking meals, from talking to her children to walking the dog. "Don't be afraid. I'm here. It's all right."

L'Engle's words echo the reassuring words Jesus says over and over again in the gospels—when he raises Jairus' daughter (Lk 8:40–56), when he comes to the apostles across the water (Mt 14:22–27), when he speaks of his impending passion and death (Jn 16:22), and when he appears to his apostles after the resurrection (Jn 20:19–29). "Don't be afraid. I'm here. It's all right."

Most of us realize we have much to be afraid of in life. We also know how little we can do to ensure the safety of those we love. But coupled with this stark realism is our consoling Christian faith—a faith which reassures us, "Don't be afraid... Jesus is here...It's all right."

Jesus, help me to speak words
of reassurance to someone today.

[103] **Throwing seed with open hands**

In one of his talks, Paul Molinari, SJ, said: "You must not be concerned about the fruit of what you do. You must be generous in throwing the seed with open hands, without becoming discouraged when the fertile soil seems scarce."

Spring is the season of the year that reminds us of this truth. We need not worry about the fruit of what we do. We need only be generous with our sowing. This is not easy. Understandably, we'd all like to see the fruit of our labors, or at least a few green shoots sprouting from the seed we've sown so painstakingly. For when we see no fruit, what happens? Perhaps we are tempted to hold back some of our seed. We ask, "Why waste my seed here?"

God, on the other hand, wants us to sow generously, extravagantly, even wastefully—wherever we may find ourselves. We can afford to, too, knowing full well that we are not the lord of the harvest. God is. We are mere sowers. As such, we need concern ourselves solely with this: how open are our hands, how wide is the arc of our throw.

Lord of the Harvest, teach me to
throw my seed with open hands.

---

[104] **A parent's love**

A few years back, I was at a mall with a nun friend of mine. It was early spring, but cold and windy. While there, we, by chance, ran into my friend's mother. After the usual exchange of warm greetings, her mother suddenly became serious. Tugging the sleeve of her daughter's jacket, she asked sternly,

"Is that jacket warm enough?"

I had to smile. My friend was no little kid. She was in her thirties and had left home years ago. But here was her mother, still worrying whether her jacket was warm enough for her. It reminded me of my own mother. When I was about eleven years old, I had a foot problem that necessitated regular trips to a foot doctor until I was seventeen. Many years later, my mother still occasionally asked me, "How are your feet, Honey?"

Do mothers ever stop worrying about their kids? Do parents ever stop being parents? I think not. When people have a child, they make a commitment for life. Once a parent, always a parent. There's no retirement. And when parents become grandparents, they start worrying about their grandchildren— and then their great-grandchildren!

A parent's love is a lot like God's love, a love that goes on and on and on.

God, help me to reflect your everlasting love.

----

[105] On aging

A friend of mine was beginning to feel a little arthritis in her joints. She said to me, "The other day I woke up and wondered, 'When did I get my mother's body?'" I, being older than she was, knew exactly what she meant.

How do we react to getting old? Do we fret? Do we deny it? Are we afraid? All of these responses are understandable. In truth, our society offers us little help for facing the aging process except pain pills, beauty creams, and cosmetic surgery.

For many, even death itself isn't as foreboding as is aging. Someone once remarked, "It's not death that I worry about. It's the process of getting old." Many of us fear that gradual process of "losing things," from our hearing to our friends. Or losing control over our finances, our bodies, our minds.

Writer Rich Heffern said, "Acceptance of aging, to me, seems like an acid test for our spirituality. Do we trust that the cosmos we come from is ultimately benign, that God is really love?" Good question.

Thank God we have individuals in our midst who are aging well—parents, aunts and uncles, friends, elderly members of our communities. These are individuals who, despite their increasing infirmity, continue to smile and laugh, to find enchantment in life, and to come up with creative ways to serve others!

God, as I continue to age, may I continue to trust that the cosmos is benign and you are really love.

———————————————⟨※⟩———————————————

[106] **The parable of the brownies**

When I was a little girl, I liked to bake things from scratch. One day, early in my baking career, I said to my brother Paul, "Today I'm going to bake you some brownies." My brother, very pleased with my announcement, went for a walk in the woods while I set about my task.

I did everything the recipe told me to do. I creamed the eggs and sugar, sifted the flour, melted the unsweetened chocolate, and mixed the batter. Finally, I proudly put the pan of brownies into the oven to bake. Several minutes later, as I was cleaning up the dishes, I was shocked by what I saw on the counter: the bowl of sifted flour! I had forgotten to put in the flour! In my naiveté, I said to myself, "Oh well, it probably won't make much of a difference," and I poured the unused flour back into the bag.

Needless to say, the absence of flour did make a difference. A big difference! When I took the pan out of the oven, there were my brownies: a thin layer of chocolate goo on the bottom of the pan. To this day, my brothers tease me about this incident—but I remind them: "You still ate them!"

What does this story have to do with Christian living? To me, it's something of a parable. In his first letter to the Corinthians, St. Paul gave us the recipe for happy living, namely, faith, hope, and love. Then he added, "And the greatest of these is love" (1 Cor 13:13). Perhaps we could also say, "And the flour in the recipe for happy living is love."

Jesus, help me to put all your ingredients into my life
—especially love.

---

[107] Silence

We live in a noisy world. Cars speed down our streets, planes soar overhead, dogs bark in the neighborhood, the TV blares in the living room, and our phones ring all hours of day and night. (As I typed that last sentence, my telephone rang!) Coupled with these obvious noises are other less noticeable ones: the steady humming of our refrigerators, furnaces, air conditioners, and computers.

In addition to these noises, we have words. Now, I, for one, love words. After all, I make part of my living off words! Yet even I am sometimes overwhelmed by all the words that bombard me in a single day, plus all the words I am compelled to generate each day.

The Trappist monks have a saying: "Speak only when it improves the silence." If only the rest of the world would live by that maxim! But the reality is, for most of us, noise and words are the norm; silence, the exception.

But just because silence is the exception, this doesn't mean we shouldn't make efforts to cultivate it in our lives on a regular basis. For most spiritual writers speak of the necessity of silence in developing a deeper relationship with God. Said one, "Only a person who can bear silence will hear the voice of God."

Although it's true God can and does sometimes speak to us through noise, it seems that God's preferred modus operandi is still silence.

God, help me to cultivate silence that I may hear your voice.

---

[108] **Good prayer**

In his book *The God Who Fell From Heaven*, Father John Shea tells the story of a woman who one day found a "sock of pot" in her fourteen-year-old son's sock drawer. Angrily, she stomped into the den where her son was watching TV and smacked him. Later, on her way to church, she met Father Shea and told him what had happened. "I can't stand to look at him," she said.

The woman then went into church and sat in a back pew for quite some time. When she emerged, Shea asked her, "How are you doing?"

"I prayed about it," she said.

Shea asked, "What did you find out?"

The woman replied, "He's not all bad and I'm not all good."

Good prayer does that. It helps us to see things differently. It invites us to compassion and humility.

God, may my prayer help me to be more compassionate and more humble.

---

[109] **An alternate perception**

I'm a morning person. As such, I sometimes do my grocery shopping quite early in the day, thus avoiding the crowds. I shared this practice with a friend of mine, a night owl. "When you go shopping at 7:00 in the morning, there are no lines at the checkout," I said proudly.

My friend grinned and said, "Melannie, there are no lines at the checkout at midnight, either!"

I had to laugh. For here I was, presuming that, by being a morning person, I somehow had an advantage over my friend. But she was quick to remind me that being a night owl gave her certain advantages, too.

The incident illustrates this: No one has the complete picture. No one has the definitive perspective on life. We need each other's viewpoint.

Broadening our perspective on life is no small thing. Rather, it lies at the core of our Christian faith. For what are faith, hope, and love except alternate perceptions of reality?

God, keep altering my perception of life!

[110] **Lent and the process of repenting**

When we think of Lent, we think of the words of John the Baptist: "Repent, for the kingdom of heaven has come near!" (Mt 3:2). The word repent means to feel regret for something. "I'm sorry I broke your toy truck," we said (or were made to say!) to our little brother. "I'm sorry I got ketchup on your blouse," we said to our teenage sister.

But repentance goes beyond expressing sorrow. It also means to turn from sin and dedicate oneself to the amendment of one's life. It demands change. But we're not talking surface change here—a new haircut, braces, losing ten pounds. No, we're talking serious change—namely, renewal.

In an article entitled "Turning Over a New Leaf," Robert Stoudt distinguishes between change and renewal. He writes, "Change pertains to exterior details, renewal to interiority." He goes on to say that change relates to "specific behaviors modified, curbed, or adapted"; whereas renewal "considers the motivations that produce the behaviors in the first place."

A good question to reflect on during Lent, then, is this: what motivations are producing the behaviors I would like to change? Fear? Hurt? Anger? Guilt? Getting to the motivational roots of my behaviors may take time. It may require help, too. But Lent offers us forty days to at least begin the process of repenting.

God, help me to identify the motivations that
produce the behaviors I wish to change.

[111] Hummingbirds

I phoned my mother to wish her a happy Mother's Day. "Guess what!" she said to me with excitement. Before I could guess, she said. "Our hummingbirds are back!"

My parents lived for twenty-five years on three acres in northeastern Ohio. And every May, my mother religiously hung a hummingbird feeder outside their kitchen window. And every May, the hummingbirds, just as religiously, showed up. From the excitement in my mother's voice, I knew the arrival of the hummingbirds was an event worthy of celebration.

I admire hummingbirds! First, they're so tiny—some not much larger than a bumblebee. Second, they go so fast! Even a slow-motion camera can't capture their rapidly beating wings. Third, they fly in any direction: up, down, frontwards, backwards, sideways. No other bird rivals them in agility.

Another reason hummingbirds intrigue me is their beauty: those flitting iridescent colors that poet Emily Dickinson describes as "A resonance of emerald,/A rush of cochineal." But perhaps I admire hummingbirds most because of their ability to migrate thousands of miles on less than an ounce of fat. And some, I've heard, actually fly across the Gulf of Mexico in one stretch!

The secret of the hummingbirds' aeronautical capabilities, of course, is that they, like most birds, travel light. It's a message we pack rats and gizmo collectors need to hear. Jesus himself said, "Do not store up for yourselves treasures on earth...but store up for yourselves treasures in heaven...For where your treasure is, there your heart will be also" (Mt 6:19–21).

God, help me to travel light.

[112] **The beckoning risen Jesus**

Many Christians prefer Christmas to Easter. That's understandable, for the Christmas story has many elements that are naturally attractive: a newborn baby, a young married couple, a mysterious star, woolly sheep, angelic choirs, and a motley group of shepherds who end up with the best seats in the house.

In contrast, what does Easter have to offer? A stone rolled back, an empty tomb, and three women running madly away, scared out of their wits. Another way of looking at the two feasts is this: at Christmas, we say "hello" to Jesus; but at Easter we seem to say "goodbye." At Easter Jesus parts company with us. For, when he rose from the dead, Jesus did not simply come back from the dead. He was not merely resuscitated. No, when he rose, he went beyond death to an intrinsically new life. And it is from there that he beckons us to follow him.

Of course, in one sense, Jesus is always here with us, yes. But in another way, he goes before us. "He is not here," the angel says to the women. "He is going ahead of you" (Mt 28:6–7). And it is imperative that we keep before us that image of a beckoning risen Jesus. Why? So that we never make the mistake of thinking we are already home.

Risen Jesus, keep beckoning me!

---

[113] **Easter surprises**

If there's one word that summarizes Easter, it's the word "Surprise!" All four evangelists, while emphasizing different aspects of the Easter story, make one thing clear: Jesus' resurrection was a big surprise not only for his enemies, but even for his closest followers.

In Mark, the three women who trek to the tomb early Sunday morning are astonished and frightened when they find the tomb empty (Mk 16:1–8). In Matthew, even when the disciples see the risen Jesus with their own eyes, they still doubt that it is really he (Mt 28:17). In Luke, the two disciples on the way to Emmaus are flabbergasted when they realize that the guy who nonchalantly joined them on their walk was actually the risen Jesus (Lk 24:13–32). And in John, Mary Magdalene doesn't have a clue that the man in the garden is Jesus until he surprises her by calling her name (Jn 20:11–18).

One fitting way to celebrate Easter, then, is to surprise people. We can begin by surprising ourselves, by doing something we don't ordinarily do. The options are almost unlimited: we could sign up for a pottery class, write a poem, learn line dancing, visit an art museum, work on our family tree, start a garden. Surprising ourselves is one way to get out of our rut or (if you will) out of our "tomb," that is, our usual way of being. What an Easter kind of thing to do!

We can also celebrate Easter by surprising others, by doing small favors around the house, the workplace, the parish, the neighborhood. We can surprise individuals with phone calls, visits, emails, or cards for no particular occasion.

Someone has said, "The simplest meaning of Easter is that we are living in a world in which God has the last word." That last word may very well be "Surprise!"

Jesus, help me to surprise myself and someone else today.

[114] **Funeral plans**

I know a number of people who have planned their own funerals. They've chosen the songs and picked a homilist and a eulogist. These folks are not seriously ill, mind you. Most of them are in good health and are likely to live for many years yet.

I, for one, have not the slightest inclination to plan my own funeral. It's not because I think such a thing is macabre. Nor am I afraid to face my own mortality. No, I refuse to plan my funeral for one basic reason: who is the funeral for, anyway?

Some might say the funeral is for the one being buried. But what need does the deceased have for a funeral? He or she is dead and has need of nothing we living can give—except perhaps a prayer or two.

I am suggesting that funerals are primarily for the mourners, the people left behind in sorrow and pain. They're the ones who need all the consolation they can get, and they can get some of that consolation by planning and celebrating their loved one's funeral. All those beautiful songs, all those consoling Scripture readings, all those powerful prayers for them to choose from.

If you feel compelled to plan your own funeral, then, by all means, go ahead. But I, for one, have crossed it off my "to do" list—forever.

God, give me a healthy awareness of the inevitability of my own death. And may that awareness influence my choices today.

[115] **The parable of the last judgment**

The parable of the last judgment (Mt 25:31–46) is a sobering one. In it, Jesus is shown dividing a gigantic herd of people into two groups: the sheep (whom he directs to his right) and the goats (to his left). Then Jesus says to the sheep, "Come, you that are blessed by my Father, inherit the kingdom prepared for you from the foundation of the world." The sheep are shocked. "Who—us?" they ask. It is clear they haven't a clue what they did to deserve this.

So Jesus tells them: "I was hungry…thirsty…a stranger… naked…sick…in prison…and you cared for me." The sheep are amazed. "But we never saw you," they protest. Then Jesus says those beautiful words, "Just as you did it to one of the least of these…you did it to me."

Then Jesus turns to the goats and says (in a nutshell), "You never cared for me when I was in need." The goats object, "But when did we see you in need?" To which Jesus says those somber words, "Just as you did not do it to one of the least of these, you did not do it to me."

Recently a friend, preaching on this passage, said, "The question we must ask ourselves is this: 'Where am I missing Jesus today?'" In other words, in which person or persons do I think Jesus isn't present? That elderly woman with Alzheimer's? That homeless man? That unborn baby? That lawyer with his briefcase? That man on death row? That bishop in his miter? That young mother on welfare? Those teenagers? Those gays? Those terrorists?

Where is Jesus today for me? Probably in the person I least expect.

Jesus, give me eyes to see you in the people I least expect.

[116] **"I want to want!"**

Shortly before Eric's sixth birthday, his grandmother asked him, "Eric, what do you need for your birthday?" Eric wrinkled up his nose and replied emphatically, "I don't want to *need*! I want to *want*!"

Though not even six, Eric already knew the difference between "need" and "want." "Need" is what you have to have—like underwear, toothpaste, green vegetables. No fun there. But "want" is what you'd like to have, and that opens up a world of unlimited possibilities—like a new bicycle, video games, chocolate candy!

Spiritual writers tell us we must distinguish between our needs and our wants, between those things essential for living and those things that aren't. Good advice, especially for those of us living in a so-called consumer society. For our consumer society works overtime trying to convince us that all our wants are really needs. It has succeeded in doing this every time we say (or think) things like this: "I have to have that _____!" (Fill in the blank with dress, car, computer, chain saw, TV, cellphone, vacation, boat, gadget, or anything else you can think of.)

There's a danger in focusing too much on satisfying only our wants. If we do, life becomes little more than a frantic pursuit for more and more things. Simultaneously, such a preoccupation distracts us from ever discovering our deeper and more vital needs—like our need for intimacy, solitude, truth, leisure, forgiveness, love—and even our need for God.

God, lead me to discover my deepest needs,
especially my need for you.

[117] Quilting: "That's what piecing is"

Theologian Dolores Leckey once gave a talk on "Women and Creativity." She told of the many pioneer women who designed and sewed all those incredibly beautiful quilts. Leckey noted that, to these women, quilting was not only "an artistic statement," it was also "a philosophical expression." She cited the words of an elderly quilter found in the book *The Quilters: Women and Domestic Art, An Oral History*. The woman begins by describing life on the frontier, and ends up talking about quilting as if living and quilting were one and the same thing. She says: "Sometimes you don't have control over the way things go....And then you're given just so much to work with in life and you have to do the best you can with what you got. That's what piecing is. The materials are passed on to you or are all you can afford to buy...your fate. But the way you put them together is your business. You can put them in any order you like."

In a way, living is like quilting. We start with those scraps of material passed on to us—our genetic makeup, our family history, our upbringing. Then we purchase other materials we can afford to buy with the talents and opportunities we've been given. And finally, we take all those pieces of material and we put them together. In any order we like. In a unique pattern of our own designing. That's what piecing is. That's what piecing a life is!

God, help me to piece together a beautiful life for you.

[118] **Draw what you see**

When I took biology in high school, we periodically examined things under the microscope—things like a strand of hair, a leaf, a drop of blood. Sometimes the teacher would say to us, "Draw what you see." Inevitably, sooner or later one of us would ask, "What's it supposed to look like?" The question always irked our teacher, who'd say something like, "Forget what it's supposed to look like and draw what you see!" But even then, some of us would peek into our textbook, find a picture of what we were looking at, and copy that picture!

Sometimes we mistrust our own experience. Maybe, over the years, we've made some big mistakes by doing just that. In addition, religion itself sometimes fostered this attitude of mistrust when it overemphasized our sinfulness and cautioned us against relying on our own thoughts or feelings. Many of us still think it's better to trust only the experience of other people—the so-called "experts" like the saints, theologians, spiritual writers, psychologists, and the like. Consequently, we turn to these people with our questions rather than exploring our own experience, instead of drawing what we see.

I'm not saying we shouldn't ask advice, seek counsel, or read books (like this one!) The experience of others can guide and enrich us. But it is never a substitute for our own experience. In fact, another's experience helps us only if it somehow illuminates our own.

It's important to reflect on our own experience, because that's where we encounter God. As someone has said, "Reality is God's home address."

God, help me to seek and find you in my own experience,
and to draw what I see.

[119] The deer principle

For five years I lived on a 180-acre estate in Middleburg, Virginia. We Sisters of Notre Dame used to own a school there, right in the middle of Virginia's famed horse country. Picture it: towering magnolia trees, rolling green pastures, thick woods, blue mountains to the west, and a driveway nine-tenths of a mile long! A lover of the outdoors, I frequently took long walks on our property. Sometimes I would spot deer along the way—usually in clumps of three or four, but occasionally even in herds of a dozen or more.

My walks amid all that beauty taught me many things. One thing I call "the deer principle." And it goes like this: Whenever I set out deliberately to see deer, I seldom saw them. But if, on the other hand, I was just strolling along with my mind on other things, presto! there they'd be! Silent, statuesque, and staring right at me. It was as if as soon as I let go of my resolve to see deer, they would oblige me with their presence!

I've experienced "the deer principle" in other areas of my life as well. Take writing. I, for one, work hard at writing—at coming up with ideas, finding the right words, and organizing what I have to say. But, I have learned, sometimes I am most creative not when I am most alert and in control, but when I am half-asleep with the reins of the day slipping out of my hands. This occurs most noticeably twice a day: those few minutes before I fall asleep at night and (even more so) before I am fully awake in the morning. Those times I am not trying to make something happen. I let go, and presto! all kinds of ideas, images, and words suddenly appear. (In fact, the idea for this reflection came to me as I lay in bed one morning.)

Does the "deer principle" apply to our spiritual lives as well? I think so. We go to prayer saying things like "I will meet God today! I will find an answer to my question! I will come up with a solution to this problem!" And what happens? Nothing! But later during the day or during the week, when we're taking a shower or stirring the chili or playing with the dog, presto! God's there, silent, statuesque, and gazing at us with amusement and affection.

God, teach me how to let go and allow you to oblige me with your presence.

———————————⟨✳⟩———————————

[120] Humorous observations about sundry items

Getting caught is the mother of invention. ❊ ROBERT BYRNE

Why is it we trust banks with our money and they don't trust us with their pens? ❊ ANONYMOUS

Stephen Spender, describing the face of W.H. Auden: "A wedding cake left out in the rain."

The nice thing about egotists is that they don't talk about other people. ❊ LUCILLE HARPER

Running is an unnatural act—except from enemies and to the bathroom. ❊ ANONYMOUS

He who laughs, lasts. ❊ MARY PETTIBONE POOLE

God, keep me laughing—to the last!

[121] The spirituality of wishing

Five-year-old Noah was touring the Luray Caverns in Virginia with his parents. At the end of the tour, they came to a crystal-clear pool of water. "This is our wishing pond," announced the guide. Noah begged his father for some coins. Taking them, he threw them into the pond and cried aloud, "I wish for a thousand toys!"

As the family exited the caverns, Noah suddenly appeared worried and anxious. "What's wrong?" his father asked. He replied somberly, "Where am I gonna put all those toys?"

Wishing is something we learn to do early in life. And with good reason, for wishing is psychologically healthy. It moves us beyond the past and the present, spurs us to set goals for the future, and encourages us to work toward their achievement.

Wishing is also important for our spiritual well-being. It puts us in touch with our incompleteness by reminding us we are never fully satisfied with who we are, what we have, and the way things are. And this is good. For every wish bears the seed for improvement. And every wish attests to our ultimate need for God.

Jesus said, "Where your treasure is, there your heart will also be" (Lk 12:34). Similarly, we could say, "Where your wishing is, there your heart is." To get a spiritual EKG, we need only ask ourselves: "What am I wishing for?"

God, may all my wishes lead to improvement—and to you!

[122] **It all depends on angle and framing**

Today I took a picture of a small, shapely pine tree enveloped in the morning mist. It took me quite some time to take the picture. I knew what I wanted (an upshot), but when I stooped to take it from that angle, I kept getting some telephone lines in the picture. Not wanting them in, I began to adjust my position—now to the left, back a little to the right, now a little lower, now a little closer—until, "Yes! That's it!" And I snapped the picture.

Taking pictures (and cropping them) always reminds me that the whole effect of the final picture rests largely on these two components: angle and framing. A good photographer is always asking, "What's the best angle to take this from?" and, "What do I intentionally wish to include and exclude?"

In life, much depends on angle and framing, too. When annoyed or disturbed by something, we can ask ourselves, "From what angle am I viewing this person, this thing, this situation?" Perhaps if I changed my point of view, I would see something I'm not seeing now. And, "What am I framing here?" Maybe there's something I should leave out of the picture, or something I should include that I'm not.

God, make me more aware of angle and framing today.
Help me get your picture.

---

[123] **Our image of the truth**

St. Julie Billiart founded the Sisters of Notre Dame in post-revolutionary France. Reading her letters, one realizes she had more than her share of problems. One problem involved some of the clergy of her day who sometimes opposed Julie and her fledgling congregation. One day Julie received a letter from one of her sisters describing how a priest had yelled at her with considerable rage. Julie wrote back, "Even though he were to shout so loudly that I could hear him from here, that good priest would not frighten me....Truth does not make so much noise."

St. Julie was on to something. What is our image of truth? Is it the blast of a thousand trumpets or the soft strains of a single flute? Is it a flashy display of fireworks or the steady flicker of a lone candle? Is it a volcano erupting high into the air or a seed cracking open deep within the soil?

Shortly before handing Jesus over to be crucified, Pilate asks him, "What is truth?" (Jn 18:38). In response to his question, Pilate doesn't get a lengthy dissertation or an impressive display of military might. He doesn't even get a halfway decent little miracle. Instead, Pilate gets silence. Only silence. But, as someone has pointed out, "There are times when nothing a person can say is so powerful as saying nothing." For the ultimate answer to Pilate's "What is truth?" is not a philosophical concept or major event; it is a person, the person standing before him: Jesus, "the way, and the truth, and the life" (Jn 14:6).

Jesus, continue to lead me to truth which
(I know) is ultimately you.

---

[124] On going to bed at night

Sometimes I think the way we go to bed at night is the way we're going to go to our death. If we go to bed fussing and stalling and puttering and refusing to leave our work, that's how we'll die: fussing and stalling and puttering and refusing to leave this world. I hope my little theory is correct, for I usually go to bed quite readily, perfectly content to leave some things unfinished. I tell myself as I crawl beneath the covers, "I'll pick up tomorrow where I left off today." I hope I'm just as ready and eager to die when the time comes: No fussing. No stalling. No regrets. No frets about leaving some things undone.

In fact, I hope when it's time for me to die, I can say: "What, God? It's time for me to go? Why, sure! I'll be right with you. After all, I've been expecting you!" Or, "You're a little earlier than I planned, God, but that's okay. I'm ready." Or, "It's about time you got here, God! What took you so long?"

God, help me to realize that I prepare for my death
by how I live my life every day.

---

[125] Sloth

The cartoon shows two elderly monks walking together. One says to the other, "At my age, sloth is the only sin I've got left!"

We don't read much about the sin of sloth anymore. In the book of Proverbs, on the other hand, we find frequent mention of sloth, sometimes called "laziness" or "idleness": "As a door turns on its hinges, so does a lazy person in bed" (Prv 26:14); "One who is slack in work is close kin to a vandal" (Prv 18:9); "The hand of the diligent will rule, while the lazy will be put to forced labor" (Prv 12:24); and, "Go to the ant, you lazybones; consider its ways, and be wise" (Prv 6:6).

Strictly speaking, the word "sloth" means more than mere

laziness or idleness. Sloth is really the sin of "acedia," which the fourth-century Christian ascetics dubbed "the noonday devil." According to theology professor Louis Cameli, acedia tempts us in three ways. First, it tempts us to return to the past, our former way of life, the way things used to be. The Israelites in the desert, for example, pined for the fleshpots of Egypt as soon as their journey became difficult (Ex 16:2–3). Second, acedia tempts us to do something other than what we have been called to do. I've known some parents, for example, who get so involved in their church that they end up neglecting their children! And third, acedia tempts us "to collapse into paralyzing sadness at the futility of it all," "it" being whatever good we are trying to do. Acedia whispers in our ear, "What's the use? You're only one person. Give it up already!"

God, help me to continue on my journey, to do what
you are calling me to do, and to never succumb to despair.

⊰✳⊱

[126] Jesus: Prince of Peace or Agitation?

Jesus is called the Prince of Peace. That is the name given him by the prophet Isaiah long before his birth: "And he is named Wonderful Counselor, Mighty God, Everlasting Father, Prince of Peace" (Is 9:6). Peace is what Jesus wishes his apostles, too, at the Last Supper: "Peace I leave with you; my peace I give to you" (Jn 14:27). It is also the first word he speaks to his anxious apostles after his resurrection: "Peace be with you" (Lk 24:36). Yet, in other places, Jesus specifically warns his followers against associating him exclusively with peace. "Do not think that I have come to bring peace to the earth" (Mt 10:34), he says. He then goes on to describe some of the possible unpeaceful consequences of believing in him—most notably, conflicts in familial relationships.

Jesus is our Prince of Peace—but not exclusively that. He is sometimes also our Prince of Agitation. For peace is not an absolute good. Sometimes it can be a cop-out or (worse yet) an abettor to evil. For example, we see a friend doing something wrong or harmful, and we say, "I'd say something, but I don't want to upset her." In other words, we choose peace rather than honesty or genuine love. Or we see a blatant injustice and say, "I'd do something about that, but I don't want to cause a fuss." Translation? "Peace at any price—even at the price of truth and goodness."

Literature promotes the notion that too much peace is not good for us. Take the magnificent poem "The Rime of the Ancient Mariner," by Samuel Taylor Coleridge. In that poem, a mighty sailing vessel gets caught in a terrible storm. Petrified, the sailors pray for relief from the violence and turmoil. Eventually, their prayer seems to be answered as their ship is blown into a perfectly peaceful sea. At first they are overjoyed. Peace at last! Calm after all that tumult! Only gradually do the men realize that this calm is no blessing at all. In fact, it means certain death for all of them. Their ship, "As idle as a painted ship/Upon a painted ocean," is stuck. It is going nowhere. They will all die.

In sailing, absolute peace and calm mean death. In the spiritual life, it is the same way. That's why Jesus, on a regular basis, comes into our lives as the Prince of Agitation, stirring our waters, messing up our ordered lives, prodding us to sail forward.

Jesus, make me more sensitive to your presence in my life— whether you come as Prince of Peace or Agitation.

[127] Taking time for the pain

There's an old Carly Simon song that says, "I haven't got time for the pain." (The song was eventually used in an aspirin commercial!) The words are those of someone who has recently experienced the pain of a broken relationship. What the song is saying is this: "I'm putting the pain of this experience behind me in order to get on with my life."

In one way, the words of the song are wise. We can't let the pain of the past prevent us from moving into the future. But in another way, the words can be dangerous if they tell us to ignore our pain. On the contrary, it is very important to take time for our pain. How? By acknowledging it to ourselves and perhaps to someone else in whom we can confide. Why? So our pain won't fester into self-pity, resentment, or even violence. Rather, so our pain will lead us to greater understanding, compassion, forgiveness, love.

In James Baldwin's book *Notes of a Native Son*, we find these insightful words: "I imagine one of the reasons people cling to their hates so stubbornly is because they sense, once hate is gone, they will be forced to deal with pain." Dealing with our pain is never easy. But if we don't, the consequences can be devastating—for ourselves and for our world.

God, help me to take time for my pain. And may it always lead me to greater understanding and love.

---

[128] Babies: one of God's greatest ideas

One of God's best ideas was babies. Just think of it. All human beings, no matter what century they're born in, no matter

119

what race, gender, or religion, all start out in life the same way: as babies. It didn't have to be that way. God could have had all of us, like the Greek goddess Athena, spring full-grown from our mother's (or father's) head. Or we all could have hatched from giant eggs at the age of twenty-one. But no. God decided all human beings would begin their earthly journey as babies—as tiny, fidgeting, cooing, screaming, drooling, defenseless babies. Why?

I don't know why. But I can speculate. For one thing, babies are lovable. I know, I know, babies aren't always lovable. Not when they cry at 3:00 in the morning, or wet their diaper (or worse), or spit carrots in your face. But despite the many unlovable things babies do, they somehow still remain lovable. Just take a baby anywhere—into a checkout line, into a church, onto a bus—and notice what happens. Immediately all heads turn. Some people instantly begin smiling or waving or speaking in "babylese." Babies wouldn't elicit such positive responses if they weren't so doggone lovable and cute!

But there's another reason why I think God came up with the idea of babies. Babies need a heck of a lot of love. They are totally dependent on other human beings for their survival. Whereas the babies of other species of animals become independent quite soon after birth (like turtles, rabbits, and hedgehogs), we human babies require many years of careful nurturing just to get us to where we can cross the street by ourselves, let alone make a living!

Consequently, as long as there are babies in the world, there's going to be a lot of loving going on. There has to be. Babies are one of the ways God keeps reminding us how important love really is. And God didn't mean just for babies either. All human beings need a heck of a lot of love no matter what their age—babies, kids, teenagers, young adults, midlifers, or senior citizens.

God liked the idea of babies so much that, at one point, God made this amazing decision: "I, myself, will become a baby, too!"

God, help me to love everyone you put into my life today—regardless of their age!

Index